Fun Facts
Part 1

Nathan Ryder

FUN FACTS – PART 1

Fact 1: There are no one- and two-cent coins in Finland. Prices must always be rounded up or down to the nearest five cents by law.

Fact 2: Netflix has over 20 million subscribers in China even though Netflix is not available in China.

Fact 3: On June 30th, 2015, there was a leap second. One second was added to the last minute of this day.

Fact 4: Helium is the only element that was not first discovered on Earth. Instead, it was discovered in 1868 in the form of previously unknown spectral lines in the light of the sun.

Fact 5: On the basis of number of viewers, Disney's Jungle Book was the most successful movie in Germany.

Fact 6: A study proved that 70 percent of women prefer to eat chocolate rather than have sex.

Fact 7: At the Marine Mammal Studies Institute, dolphins have been trained to get the audiences waste out of the basin. Each time they hand out trash to the animal attendants, they get food for it.

Fact 8: In 2012, the author of the book series "Fifty Shades of Grey" - E. L. James - was the most successful author of the year.

Fact 9: Before there were trees on the earth, our planet was covered by giant mushrooms.

Fact 10: Nearly 65 percent of all autistic people are left-handed.

Fact 11: Tsutomu Yamaguchi was working in Hiroshima when the first atomic bomb hit the city. As he was driving home to Nagasaki the second bomb hit. He is currently 90 years old and still alive.

Fact 12: Since the end of the Second World War, Japan has apologized in official statements more than 50 times for its acts during the war.

Fact 13: Regions of the earth where the inhabitants clearly exceed the average life expectancy of the world population are called "Blue Zones". Currently, only five Blue Zones are known worldwide. These are Okinawa (Japan), Sardinia (Italy), Nicola (Costa Rica), Ikaria (Greece) and Loma Linda (California). The reason why people there live so long is not clear.

Fact 14: Over an investigation period from 1985 to 2012, scientists were able to show that Greenland is the country with the highest suicide rate. During this period, 83 out of 100,000 people committed suicide, while 20 percent of the population reported to have attempted suicide at least once before.

Fact 15: Due to their fine and extensive root network, forest mushrooms absorb heavy metals in large quantities. That is why you should not eat more than 250 grams of forest mushrooms per week.

Fact 16: In 2014, Englishman Rory Curtis woke from a coma and thought he was the actor Matthew McConaughey.

Fact 17: The song "Hey ya" by Outkast says "Shake it like a Polaroid picture", forced Polaroid to release a press release that shaking a Polaroid too much can damage the picture.

Fact 18: As traffic in Bangkok has become so bad, the city has started to train special mobile obstetricians to help women give birth when they cannot make it to hospital on time.

Fact 19: Microsoft sued the student Mike Rowe after he launched the site MikeRowSoft.com.

Fact 20: The word Jedi from Star Wars comes from the Japanese word "Jidai-geki", which is a Japanese term for samurai movies.

Fact 21: If Coca Cola was served without colorants, it would be green and not black.

Fact 22: Strawberries are not berries, but in fact nuts.

Fact 23: The medical term for headaches due to eating too much ice-cream is sphenopalatine ganglioneuralgia.

Fact 24: Hans Zimmer has composed the soundtracks for "Lion King", "Gladiator", "Pirates of the Caribbean", "Inception" and for the "Dark Night" trilogy. According to him he had spent two weeks in a music class during his childhood and learned the rest by himself.

Fact 25: For safety reasons, the Guinness Book of World Records does not accept record attempts on how long a person can stay awake. The last registered record dates back to 1964 and is eleven days and 25 minutes.

Fact 26: When physicist Niels Bohr won the Nobel Prize, the Carlsberg Brewery gave him a house right next to the brewery with a beer pipe leading directly from the brewery into the house. Until the end of his life, Niels Bohr could drink as much beer as he wanted free of charge.

Fact 27: Jeanne Calment holds the world record as the longest living human being. She was the first person to verifiably live to celebrate her 116th to 122nd birthday. She was born in 1875, saw the Eiffel Tower being built, sold paint brushes to Vincent van Gogh and died in 1997 at the age of 122.

Fact 28: With an estimated fortune of around 23 billion dollars, Ingvar Kamprad, the founder of Ikea, was one of the richest people in the world. However, people close to him say that he still took the bus, lived in a small house and only ever booked economy flights.

Fact 29: In chess, there is a way to checkmate your opponent in two moves. If a player wins with this strategy, it is called a "Fool's Mate".

Fact 30: If you keep on walking north long enough, you will eventually be walking south. If, however, you keep on walking east, you will never be moving west.

Fact 31: In order to make wolf puppies urinate, their mother has to lick their bellies with her warm tongue.

Fact 32: The guide dog Kirsch has an honorary master's degree because he attended all lectures together with his owner.

Fact 33: The PlayStation 1 controller sold in North America was about ten percent larger than the controller sold in Japan, as Japanese people on average have smaller hands than North Americans.

Fact 34: Donald Duck's second name is "Fauntleroy".

Fact 35: At birth, a blue whale is already 26 feet long and weighs more than eight tons. In its first year, the newborn gains approximately 176 pounds of weight per day - 7.3 pounds per hour.

Fact 36: For a long time, it was tradition in Ireland that one liter of Guinness beer was given for each liter of donated blood.

Fact 37: In the last 150 years, the average body size of a human has increased by four inches.

Fact 38: The largest crossroads in the world is in China. It runs over five levels, has 20 exits and covers 99 acres.

Fact 39: Irv Gordon holds the record for the longest distance a person has ever driven in the same car. He bought a Volvo P1800 in 1966 and has driven more than 3,2 million miles since then.

Fact 40: In the Trevi Fountain in Rome 3,000 Euros is thrown in by tourists every day.

Fact 41: In Singapore, it is forbidden to chew gum. Only a few people are allowed to do so for medical reasons.

Fact 42: It is now assumed that the United States carried out a total of 638 assassination attempts on Fidel Castro. Among other things, these included poisoned cigars, contaminated diving equipment, an exploding cigar and a poisoned ballpoint pen.

Fact 43: Muhammad Ali is the only famous person whose star on the "Walk of Fame" is not on the sidewalk itself but on the wall of a building. He did not want people trampling on his name.

Fact 44: Dwayne "The Rock" Johnson has a cousin - Tanoai Reed - who has a similar physique as the actor and also resembles him fairly closely in the face. Because of this, he has been his stunt double in all his movies for over 13 years.

Fact 45: The term "money laundering" can be traced back to Al Capone, as he used Laundromats for this purpose.

Fact 46: Before English became the dominant language in the U.S., German was the second most common language.

Fact 47: The bone density of people with a mutated LRP5 gene is eight times higher than in normal people. For these people, it is virtually impossible to suffer a fracture in a normal way.

Fact 48: The deepest gold mine in the world is located in South Africa, and is situated 2.5 miles below the surface.

Fact 49: The first graphics-enabled web browser was developed in 1993.

Fact 50: In the 90s, 50 percent of all CDs produced were the free AOL Internet CD.

Fact 51: More than 50% if the world's French speaking population lives in Africa.

Fact 52: The largest Bolivian prison, San Pedro in La Paz, has developed its own society. There are no guards in the prison, and the prisoners organize all aspects of their lives themselves. There are shops and restaurants run by the prisoners, and at regular intervals the inmates even elect a new leader.

Fact 53: The Wall of China cannot be seen from space - however, China's smog can.

Fact 54: If you twist both index fingers very slowly in a clockwise motion and then move them faster, the circles suddenly move in the opposite direction.

Fact 55: The clitoris has more than 8,000 nerve endings, while the penis just has 4,000.

Fact 56: Finland has hosted the official "Wife Carrying World Championship" since 1992. In this competition, men carry their wives as fast as possible over a long obstacle course. In the end, the winner receives his wife's weight in beer.

Fact 57: Ransom payments to abductors can be written off as taxes in Germany.

Fact 58: Sound spreads through steel about 15 times faster than through air.

Fact 59: Oxford University is older than the civilization of the Aztecs.

Fact 60: Carrots were purple until the 17th century. The orange color is only a specially cultivated form that has prevailed over the past few centuries.

Fact 61: All scenes of the children of Ted Mosby in "How I Met Your Mother" were shot during the first season.

Fact 62: Before she became famous, the singer "Pink" worked for McDonald's.

Fact 63: To date, it is not clear why people and other animals need sleep. There are many theories, but even experts are uncertain about their accuracy.

Fact 64: There are more people in New York City with access to internet than people in Africa with internet connections.

Fact 65: When the game "Twister" was released in 1966, it was described as "sex in a box".

Fact 66: The original name of "Bank of America" was "Bank of Italy".

Fact 67: There's only one country between Finland and North Korea: Russia.

Fact 68: Valentina Tereshkova, sent into space in 1963, was the first woman in space. To this day, she remains the only woman to have been on a space mission alone. She was alone in space for a total of three days and orbited the Earth a total of 48 times.

Fact 69: The chimpanzee "Congo" was able to draw abstract works of art. Even Pablo Picasso was a fan of his pictures.

Fact 70: In Lapland, the horns of reindeers are sprayed with reflective color so that they can be seen better in the dark and car accidents can be prevented.

Fact 71: Your hearing is worse when you are well fed.

Fact 72: In New York City, 6,000 people die every year as a result of obesity.

Fact 73: In Denmark, there is a tradition that if you are not married by your 25th birthday, your friends and family will shower you with cinnamon.

Fact 74: "Banzai Skydiving" is an extreme sport where a parachutist first throws his parachute out of the plane and then jumps after it.

Fact 75: The Chupa Chups logo was designed by Salvador Dali.

Fact 76: It has been established that whenever actress Anne Hathaway is trending in social media, automated investment bank trading algorithms automatically buy more shares in Berkshire Hathaway.

Fact 77: In 1889, the pharmaceutical company Bayer sold the drug diacetylmorphine, which was marketed as a remedy for morphine addicts. Nowadays, the drug is better known as "heroin".

Fact 78: George Washington was known to convince voters with the help of alcohol. At an election campaign with over 400 people, he brought over 500 liters of alcohol to secure their votes.

Fact 79: Nintendo originally did not develop consoles and video games, but rather started off producing playing cards.

Fact 80: During the so called "scramble for Africa" all of Africa was colonized by foreign powers, except for Liberia and Ethiopia.

Fact 81: Porn actress Lisa Sparxxx holds the world record for the highest number of sex partners within 24 hours. In 2004, during her attempt to set a new record, she had sex with 919 different men in one day.

Fact 82: Pornhub once started a campaign called "Save the Boobs". For every 30th view in the category "small tit" or "big tit", the company donated one penny to the "Susan G Komen Foundation" - a foundation whose aim it is to cure breast cancer. However, the foundation refused the donation. Therefore, Pornhub tripled the amount of money and donated it to a foundation with a similar purpose.

Fact 83: In 2000, Michael Jackson was included in the Guinness Book of World Records as the most philanthropic musician of all time. During his career he donated more than 300 million dollars, and during his tours he visited hospitals and orphanages to give presents to the children.

Fact 84: For his role as Harry Potter, actor Daniel Radcliffe received a total pay of 74 million pounds. According to his own account, the actor has spent almost none of the money so far.

Fact 85: The Hard Rock Cafe T-shirts are the world's best-selling T-shirts.

Fact 86: The copyright to the song "Happy birthday to you" expired in 2016 in the USA and in 2017 in the European Union. Until then, royalties had to be paid to Warner Music whenever the song was played on radio or television or in a cinema.

Fact 87: Zebras and ostriches often stay together in the wilderness. Ostriches can see enemies at long distances, while zebras are able to hear enemies from far away.

Fact 88: It has been scientifically proven that your nose actually grows when you lie. Scientists refer to this as the "Pinocchio effect".

Fact 89: When in 1940 Adolf Hitler banned the public display of colored people in Germany, he was the first state leader to take action against the so-called "human zoos".

Fact 90: About 90 percent of all lung cancer cases are caused by smoking.

Fact 91: One study has shown that black humor can indicate a particularly high IQ.

Fact 92: As a student at Columbia University, Ken Hechtman stole uranium-238. He later broke into Area 51, became a reporter and after the events of 9/11 illegally entered Afghanistan, where he was ultimately taken hostage by the Taliban.

Fact 93: Shakuntala Devi holds the world record in mental arithmetic. In 1980 a computer randomly chose the two 13-digit numbers 7,686,369,774,870 and 2,465,099,745,779, which Devi had to multiply. It took her only 28 seconds for the correct answer: 18,947,668,117,995,426,462,773,730!

Fact 94: "Snakes Venom" is the strongest beer in the world with an alcohol content of 67.5 percent. It contains more alcohol than whiskey.

Fact 95: In Japan, it is socially acceptable to sleep while working. It is perceived as a sign of hard work.

Fact 96: The largest cinema in the world is the Kinépolis in Madrid, with a total of 25 different screening rooms and 9,200 seats.

Fact 97: "Steve Jobs" is the name of an Italian fashion label. The company behind the brand was founded in 2012 by two brothers after they had realized that Apple had never secured the rights to the name "Steve Jobs".

Fact 98: Our blood accounts for seven percent of our body weight.

Fact 99: A study has shown that the brain can remember things on paper more easily than their digital equivalent.

Fact 100: The Scully effect is the term used to describe the fact that after the TV series "The X-Files" was broadcast, women became increasingly interested in scientific professions. The reason for this was the female protagonist Dana Scully, who solved curious cases for the FBI thanks to her medical studies.

Fact 101: Because of the large amount of sugar in it, it is impossible for honey to spoil. Even in 1,000 years it would still be edible.

Fact 102: Hippopotamus kill more Africans than lions, crocodiles and white sharks combined.

Fact 103: The names of the main characters in the film "Inception" are Dom, Robert, Eames, Arthur, Mal and Saito. When you combine the initial letters of these names, you get the word "Dreams".

Fact 104: During World War II, the U.S. Army collaborated with Walt Disney to develop a gas mask that looked like Mickey Mouse, in order to make children less afraid of a poison gas attack.

Fact 105: The Golden Gate Bridge has to be painted regularly. The salt water corrodes the paint so fast, that one has to start repainting the bridge as soon as one is finished painting it.

Fact 106: The most common fracture in the human body is the collarbone.

Fact 107: Frequently asked questions at a Microsoft job interview are: "Why are manhole covers round?" and "Design a coffee machine that can be used by astronauts".

Fact 108: Fifty Shades of Grey began as erotic fan fiction about the main characters of Twilight: Bella and Edward.

Fact 109: The mineral "Tanzanite" is a gemstone that is mined exclusively in the Gilewy Hills near Arusha in Tanzania. This makes the gems rarer than diamonds.

Fact 110: There are so many languages in the world that it is not known how many there currently are. Scientists believe that there are more than 6,500 to 7,000 different languages.

Fact 111: US President John F. Kennedy was a passionate smoker. In 1962, he instructed his press officer to buy 1,000 Cuban cigars for him. Shortly after receiving the cigars, he went on to pass a law prohibiting the import of communist goods into the United States.

Fact 112: The grapefruit was actually an accident. It was developed by chance from a cross between pomelos and oranges.

Fact 113: Arnold Schwarzenegger was meant to play the role of Kyle Reese in the movie "Terminator".

Fact 114: In 1983, 90 percent of US media were still in the hands of 50 different companies. Today, only six companies control 90 percent of the media landscape in the USA.

Fact 115: Adolescents are increasingly suffering from sleep deprivation. The reason for this is, among other things, the early start of school.

Fact 116: The Arabic number system used around the globe today was originally developed in India and was only disseminated throughout the world by Arabic researchers.

Fact 117: An average vagina is three to four inches deep and can increase by up to 200 percent when the woman is aroused.

Fact 118: Afrikaans is the youngest language in the world. It was not officially recognized as an independent language until 1925.

Fact 119: In northern Finland, the sun never sets from June to July - it shines all day long. In winter, however, the opposite is the case. The sun never rises and the sky is at best only bathed in a dark blue.

Fact 120: Google's first tweet was "I'm 01100110 01100101 01100101 01101100 01101001 01101110 01100111 00100000 01101100 01110101 01100011 01101011 01111001 00001010" which is binary code for "I'm feeling lucky".

Fact 121: The concept of "rap battles" dates back to the fifth century. At that time, poets competed against each other in a public competition in which they rhymed insults and sexual perversions. This tradition was particularly popular in Nordic and Celtic cultures. There are stories about the Nordic god Loki, who insulted other gods in rhyme form, and even William Shakespeare refers to this in some of his plays.

Fact 122: The largest ant colony in the world was discovered in 2002 and contains several billion animals. The superstate has many millions of nests and stretches over 3,580 miles from the Italian Riviera to the northwest of Spain.

Fact 123: A positive pregnancy test in men may indicate testicular cancer.

Fact 124: Similar to the fingerprint, each human has an individual tongue print.

Fact 125: Multimillionaire Forrest Fenn, hid a treasure worth two million dollars in the Rocky Mountains. In order to find it, you have to solve a number of puzzles. Until today, nobody has found the treasure.

Fact 126: In winter, the rotor blades of wind turbines are heated so that no ice forms on them.

Fact 127: Spain and Morocco are only separated by 9 miles (15km).

Fact 128: When the Egyptians built the pyramids, there were still mammoths roaming the earth.

Fact 129: A Pinocchio paradox arises when Pinocchio says "My nose is currently growing" and is an example of the more general liar paradox. This refers to a sentence that describes its own statement as false, such as "This sentence is false."

Fact 130: On 9 August 1965, Singapore was officially expelled from Malaysia, making it the first country to involuntarily gain independence.

Fact 131: Hulk originally was meant to be a grey monster but as the printing works had problems to always use the identical shade of grey, the creators decided to turn Hulk green.

Fact 132: The International Space Station is the most expensive object ever made by humans. It has cost 160 billion dollars so far.

Fact 133: Ring announcer Michael Buffer had his famous phrase "Let's get ready to rumble" trademarked back in 1992. To date, this has earned him more than 400 million dollars.

Fact 134: Vagina is the Latin word for "sheath".

Fact 135: The name "England" derives from the old English term "Englaland", which means "Land of the Angles".

Fact 136: In 1967, a former Prime Minister of Australia disappeared without a trace and has still not been found.

Fact 137: One bite of the Inland-Taipans - the most poisonous snake in the world - injects enough poison into its victim to kill more than 230 people.

Fact 138: High heels were originally worn by men to look taller. It was only in the 17th century that women began to wear such shoes in order to be more masculine. The result was that men were no longer wearing high heels, so as not to look feminine.

Fact 139: George Lucas obtained the rights to the word "droid". When Motorola released a cell phone with this name, they had to pay a fee to George Lucas.

Fact 140: The avocado core is also edible and contains even more nutrients than the pulp.

Fact 141: So far about 270 people have had their bodies frozen, to be revived in the future.

Fact 142: There is no city that is more often destroyed in movies than New York.

Fact 143: The reason why actor Morgan Freeman wears earrings is due to a maritime tradition. They wore their earrings, so that their own burial could be paid with them, in case of their death.

Fact 144: No mammal can dive deeper than Cuvier's beaked whale. A dive into the depth of the oceans can last up to 140 minutes and, according to measurements, reach a depth of 9,816 feet.

Fact 145: In order to avoid a long-standing dispute, the CEO's of Southwest Airline and Stevens Aviation decided to resolve their problem by arm wrestling. The winner was given the right to use a specific advertising slogan.

Fact 146: The Norwegian Hans Lengseth holds the record for the world's longest beard. His beard had a total length of 17.5 feet.

Fact 147: From 1920 onwards, Alexander Alexandrovich Bogdanov tried to discover a medical fountain of youth by performing blood transfusions on himself and injecting himself with the blood of younger people. One blood transfusion, however, was contaminated with malaria and tuberculosis, which eventually killed Bogdanov.

Fact 148: In ancient Greece the sandals of prostitutes bared an inscription, so that the words "follow me" appeared on the sandy ground.

Fact 149: In the history of Mexico, on one occasion, there were three presidents on one day.

Fact 150: To avoid baggage fees, a man from China wore 70 items of clothing on his body.

Fact 151: In 1916, a law was submitted to the US Congress to stipulate that any declaration of war by the USA first had to be confirmed by a referendum and that anyone who voted "yes" would have to go to war themselves. However, the law was never passed.

Fact 152: After the great success of the Eiffel Tower, London planned the construction of the similar looking Watkin's Tower in 1892. Due to economic difficulties encountered by the construction company, however, the tower was never completed and was later demolished. At over 1.148 feet, it would have been the tallest building of its time.

Fact 153: If you bathe in alcohol, you can get drunk.

Fact 154: Tattooing is illegal in South Korea. In the country, tattoos are mainly worn by criminals, which is why a tattoo is considered a valid reason for a company not to hire somebody.

Fact 155: February 29 was first introduced as a leap day by Julius Caesar in 45 BC.

Fact 156: The first president of Zimbabwe was President Canaan Banana.

Fact 157: With a height of 59 feet, the tallest animal to ever have lived on earth was probably the Sauroposeidon. One of its cervical vertebrae alone was already 4.6 feet long.

Fact 158: The more you burp, the less you have to fart.

Fact 159: In 2001, a study concluded that murder was the most common cause of death among pregnant women in the United States between 1993 and 1998.

Fact 160: A dog's sense of smell is 10,000 times stronger than that of a human being.

Fact 161: The name of the Microsoft search engine "Bing" comes from the word "Bingo", which you shout out when you get exactly the answer you had hoped for.

Fact 162: If you visit a Jewish grave, it is common practice to leave a small stone as a symbol of mourning and remembrance. The tradition dates back to a time when all Jewish graves were still in the desert. In order to prevent scavengers from digging up the corpses, the mourners erected pyramids of small stones.

Fact 163: It is impossible to draw a six while turning your foot clockwise simultaneously.

Fact 164: There are approximately sever million tons of plastic waste in our oceans. Just by doing without plastic bags, people could significantly improve the situation.

Fact 165: The most frequently visited tourist attraction in Paris is not the Eiffel Tower or the Louvre, but Disneyland.

Fact 166: The Italian state of Bellagio, namesake of the Las Vegas hotel with the same name, has fewer inhabitants than the hotel has rooms.

Fact 167: During the Cold War, the Soviet Union launched the "Intervision Song Contest", the Soviet equivalent of the Eurovision Song Contest. However, since not every viewer had a telephone to vote on, the audience instead had to turn on the lights in their houses, if they liked the song, and turn them off, if they didn't. The local power station then used the electricity consumption to determine how many people had voted for a song.

Fact 168: In Iran 70 percent of all science students are female.

Fact 169: Anthony Hopkins won an Oscar for Best Actor for his portrayal of Hannibal Lector in The Silence of the Lambs, although he only appeared in the movie for less than 17 minutes.

Fact 170: On average, each major character of "How I Met Your Mother" earned 120,000 dollars per episode. Barney Stinson actor Neil Patrick Harris earned 210,000 dollars per episode.

Fact 171: The first dinosaur bones were not discovered and scientifically described until 1824. So before that, people never knew that dinosaurs used to roam our planet.

Fact 172: Alcohol protects against radiation.

Fact 173: Excessive sleep deprivation can lead to obesity.

Fact 174: A substitute for cling film made of crab shells and plant fibers was developed in the United States.

Fact 175: The large yellow "M" in the McDonald's logo does not actually represent an "M", but rather the two original characteristic arches of McDonald's restaurants.

Fact 176: In 1994 a man was arrested in Los Angeles for scaring elderly people. He dressed himself as the grim reaper and looked inside the windows of the elderly.

Fact 177: The brain growth of early humans only began due to the increased protein intake from an increasingly meat-oriented diet.

Fact 178: The first Game Boy had as much computing power needed as for the first moon landing.

Fact 179: The Atlantic Ocean is saltier than the Pacific Ocean.

Fact 180: March 14th is the day of the number Pi. In the English notation 3/14, the date corresponds to the first three digits of the number.

Fact 181: In terms of GDP growth, Ethiopia was the fastest growing economy in the world in 2017.

Fact 182: In France it is prohibited by law, to name a pig "Napoleon".

Fact 183: Kirani James was the first Olympian to win a gold medal for his home country Grenada. His homeland was so proud of it that there was a huge celebration for him and he was rewarded with over 220,000 euros. Today he can even be found on the country's stamps, a stadium bears his name and his hometown opened a museum about his achievements.

Fact 184: The gravity on the moon is about one-sixth of the earth's gravitational pull.

Fact 185: The sun is actually white. But our atmosphere makes it look yellowish to us.

Fact 186: Even though he is already dead, Michael Jackson has earned more than 100,000,000 dollars per year in the last seven years. In monetary terms, his most successful year was 2016, when he earned a total of over 825,000,000 dollars.

Fact 187: Because of the reduced distance to the central core of the earth at the equator, people at the equator weigh less than people at the poles.

Fact 188: Uranus is 63 times larger than Earth.

Fact 189: American professional basketball player Shaquille O'Neal scored only a single three-point shot throughout his entire professional career.

Fact 190: "Cunningham's Law" describes the phenomenon that the fastest way to find a correct answer on the Internet is not to ask the question, but to post the wrong answer.

Fact 191: One gram of DNA contains as much information as could be stored on 600 billion traditional CDs.

Fact 192: The indents on a golf ball are called "dimples".

Fact 193: Some cities in the United States have started spraying Christmas trees still standing in the woods in winter with fox urine. It is odorless while frozen, but smells awful as soon as it melts. This is to prevent tree thieves from going into the forest to cut down a Christmas tree on their own.

Fact 194: The colder your bedroom is, the higher is the likelihood of having a nightmare.

Fact 195: The video game "Super Mario Bros." was so popular in 1985 that the best-selling book in Japan was a guidebook containing tips on how best to play the game.

Fact 196: The deepest hole ever explored by man was 7.5 miles deep. Compared to that, the earth has a diameter of 7,926 miles.

Fact 197: The human brain consumes about 20 percent of the body's total energy.

Fact 198: The Small World Phenomenon states that every person on the planet is connected to every other person through a short chain of only six acquaintances

Fact 199: The 2022 World Soccer Championship will be opened in Lusail (Qatar), a city which did not exist till recently.

Fact 200: In his youth, Che Guevara boasted to not have washed his T-shirt for at least 25 weeks.

Fact 201: "Bart Gets an F" - the first episode of the second season of "The Simpsons", is the most watched Simpsons episode.

Fact 202: The official length of a marathon was defined as 26,219 miles because it was exactly the length of the course at the Olympic Games in London in 1908 and not because it corresponds to the historical distance between Athens and Marathon. That distance is only about 24.8 miles.

Fact 203: Nuclear divers are professional divers who carry out repair and cleaning work in the water of the cooling systems of nuclear reactors.

Fact 204: In 1911, the Niagara Falls froze completely.

Fact 205: More than 90 percent of China's inhabitants say they do not believe in a god, making China the most unbelieving country in the world.

Fact 206: In the earth's core, there are temperatures of up to 10,800 degrees Fahrenheit.

Fact 207: To prepare for her tour, Beyoncé always sings while jogging.

Fact 208: The South African rock hyrax is only 20 inches tall, weighs about 8.8 pounds and looks like a big guinea pig. Nevertheless, its closest relative is the elephant.

Fact 209: At the geographically most northern point on earth, every line you draw points south.

Fact 210: In 1755, Lisbon was hit by a strong earthquake that destroyed almost all the Catholic churches in the city, while all the city's brothels remained largely intact. The event ushered in a long-lasting crisis of faith in Portugal.

Fact 211: Chinatown in New York is the largest settlement of Chinese citizens outside Asia.

Fact 212: Every year around 600 lightning bolts strike the Statue of Liberty.

Fact 213: Jonas Salk refused to take out a patent on his polio vaccine. He commented that: "There is no patent. Could you patent the sun?"

Fact 214: There are an estimated 500 million dogs on our planet.

Fact 215: A Rubik's Cube with three times three pieces offers 43,252,003,274,489,856,000 different combinations.

Fact 216: Foxes use the Earth's magnetic field to estimate distances.

Fact 217: In Cambodia you can buy pizzas with marijuana as a topping. It is called Happy Pizza.

Fact 218: If one took all the world's water and placed it into a cube, it would accommodate 39,375 cubic feet.

Fact 219: "Nomophobia" describes the fear of not being available via mobile phone.

Fact 220: The 100 richest people in the world earned so much money last year that they could end global poverty four times over.

Fact 221: In Australia in 2009, snipers were tasked with defending a colony of penguins against possible enemies to guarantee the survival of this rare penguin species.

Fact 222: In 1998, Marvel offered Sony the film rights for all its superheroes for only 25 million dollars. Sony rejected the deal, however, and only bought the rights to Spider Man for ten million dollars, believing that the viewers would only be interested in this character.

Fact 223: "Point Nemo" is the place on the earth's surface that is furthest away from any mainland or island. It is located in the southern Pacific Ocean, 1,670 miles from the nearest mainland. Even the astronauts on the ISS space station are closer to this point than any other person on the mainland anywhere.

Fact 224: There is 4G reception on Mount Everest.

Fact 225: An ostrich can run a marathon in less than 60 minutes.

Fact 226: If you were to stack all the viruses in the world on top of each other, this would result in a tower that would extend far beyond the moon, even further than our sun, further than Alpha Centauri and further than the edge of the Milky Way and into the next galaxy, with a total height of about 200 million light years.

Fact 227: There are butterflies that migrate south every winter, just like birds. Every autumn, the monarch butterfly sets off on its journey from the north of the United States to Mexico, covering a distance of 2,175 miles. Every day, they cover between 44 and 186 miles.

Fact 228: The true inventor of the first practical light bulb was not Thomas Alva Edison, but Joseph Wilson Swan. He had already secured a patent for his invention in England two years before Edison. But the two eventually reached an out-of-court agreement and joined forces in the Edison & Swan United Electric Light Company.

Fact 229: The Japanese giant crab is the largest living crab and can reach a span of up to 12.1 feet. However, the body has an average diameter of only 14.6 inches.

Fact 230: The actor Mark Wahlberg was suspended from school after just a few years and therefore never finished it. To be a shining example to his kids, he catched up on his high school diploma in the age of 42.

Fact 231: In its language selection, Facebook offers the language "pirate".

Fact 232: Ten percent of all Germans don't know why they celebrate Christmas.

Fact 233: Thursday is named after the Nordic god of thunder "Thor".

Fact 234: In the 1940s, the Coca Cola Company developed a colorless version of Coca Cola specifically for the USSR.

Fact 235: People with creative professions have higher life expectancies than people with other professions.

Fact 236: During the day, clouds are higher up in the sky than during the night.

Fact 237: Pablo Escobar - the world's biggest drug lord - had so much cash that he had to spend 2,500 dollars a month on rubber bands that held his money together.

Fact 238: African American Ebbie Tolbert was born in 1807 and lived in slavery for more than 50 years. At the advanced age of 113 years - shortly before her death - she was allowed to cast her ballot for the first time in her life in St. Louis.

Fact 239: With 2.3 million soldiers, China has the largest army in the world. The USA follows in second place with 1.4 million.

Fact 240: In order to die of a caffeine overdose, a person would have to consume about 100 cups of coffee in a very short time.

Fact 241: Studies show that doctors who play video games perform surgical procedures more precisely than other doctors.

Fact 242: An interesting new pattern of behavior was observed in Japanese crows. Nuts, which the animals are not able to crack on their own, are increasingly thrown onto roads by the crows so that cars drive over them and crack them. Afterwards, the crow flies back to the open nut and collects the contents.

Fact 243: Annually, more people die from being hit by a champagne cork than from the bite of a venomous spider.

Fact 244: Because the movie "Psycho" was produced in black-and-white, chocolate syrup was used for blood.

Fact 245: In preparation for his role as Walter White in "Breaking Bad" Bryan Cranston was taught by the DEA how to make meth.

Fact 246: Beavers have orange teeth, as they contain a lot of iron. The mineral makes the teeth particularly resistant to external forces.

Fact 247: The classic film "One flew over the cuckoo's nest" with Jack Nicholson was actually shot in a mental hospital. Many of the patients featured in the movie were actually being treated there at the time.

Fact 248: In the middle of Lake Taal on the island of Luzan, which belongs to the Philippines, lies Volcano Island, which is home to a crater lake which in turn contains a small island called Volcano Point. It is therefore an island in a lake on an island in a lake on an island.

Fact 249: Every year on 13 October, Finland celebrates the official day of failure.

Fact 250: McDonald's is the biggest customer of Coca Cola.

Fact 251: In addition to humans, homosexuality has been discovered in over 1,500 animal species. Same sex love is therefore anything but contrary to nature.

Fact 252: In 1990, the Michigan police organized a wedding of two of their undercover agents. Numerous drug dealers have been invited and were arrested during the wedding ceremony.

Fact 253: A Geiger counter clicks when it is exposed to radioactivity because the radiation releases electrons from the noble gas in the counter tube. This causes a chain reaction, resulting in a brief flow of electrical current, which is made audible via a loudspeaker.

Fact 254: The leaves of the "skeleton flower" become transparent when they come into contact with rain.

Fact 255: In France people were killed by the guillotine up until 1977.

Fact 256: In Uganda there is a kingdom called Buganda and its national language is Luganda.

Fact 257: Termite queens have the longest life expectancy of all insects. They can live up to 50 years.

Fact 258: The longest limousine in the world is almost 102 feet long and has 26 wheels. It is equipped with a king-size waterbed, a small helicopter landing pad and a swimming pool.

Fact 259: American Express credit card numbers always start with a three, Visa cards with a four, Mastercards with a five and Discover Cards with a six.

Fact 260: Pac-Man was originally named "Puck Man"

Fact 261: "Lifetime" paid 750,000 dollars per episode for the worldwide distribution rights on the TV show "How I Met Your Mother".

Fact 262: Schools test only your memory and not your intelligence.

Fact 263: The "Like" button on Facebook was originally supposed to be called the "Awesome" button.

Fact 264: The brain takes about 0.6 seconds to choose the right word for a term.

Fact 265: Geo-engineering refers to the use of technical means to influence chemical processes on Earth. In order to limit global warming, one of the topics discussed in this field of research is the introduction of reflecting particles into the atmosphere to partially reflect incoming solar rays.

Fact 266: If you enter "Beam me up, Scotty" as a search term on YouTube, all videos are "beamed" to the screen.

Fact 267: Female skunks are able to influence the development of their embryos, in order to delay birth in times of food shortages.

Fact 268: In 2018, a message in a bottle was found in Australia which had been dropped into the Indian Ocean by a German research vessel in 1886.

Fact 269: Goosebumps are a reflex from the times when man had much more hair. When our hair stands up, we appeared bigger and more menacing to enemies.

Fact 270: If you dissolve Viagra in water and give it to your plants, they remain fresh up to a week longer.

Fact 271: Since 1989, the mass of all living insects has decreased by around 76 percent: The causes could be too much fertilizer in agriculture, a reduction in the amount of available green space and climate change.

Fact 272: From 1912 to 1948 architecture was an Olympic discipline.

Fact 273: Just five percent of all babies suck their left thumb. The remaining 95 percent use their right one.

Fact 274: Netflix now accounts for about 15 percent of all Internet traffic in the United States.

Fact 275: About 90 percent of people won't find the the mistake   in   here: A,B,C,D,E,F,G,H,I,J,K,L,M,N,O,P,Q,R,S,T,U,V,W,X,Y,Z.

Fact 276: Taiwan was the first country to provide free Wi-Fi to all citizens.

Fact 277: There are about nine million people in a prison around the world. 25 percent of them come from the USA.

Fact 278: Man has already left over 200 tons of garbage on the moon, including 70 spaceships, backpacks, 96 bags with urine and vomit as well as old boots.

Fact 279: Robert Lane named his two sons "Winner" and "Loser". Winner Lane turned criminal, while Loser Lane had a successful career at the NYPD.

Fact 280: James Harrison is a record holder in blood donations. He donated his blood over 1,000 times.

Fact 281: In 1856 a man from Havana took off in his hot air balloon and was never seen again.

Fact 282: After the breeding season, swifts spend up to ten months in the air without landing a single time. With that, they hold the record among birds.

Fact 283: 50,000 people die a year in the U.S. from the effects of passive smoking.

Fact 284: African-American Madam C. J. Walker, born in 1867 as Sarah Breedlove, developed a hair care product for black women that sold extremely well, making her the first female millionaire in the United States.

Fact 285: When Queen Elizabeth visited the set of "Game of Thrones", she was asked if she would like to sit on the Iron Throne. However, she declined, as she is not allowed to sit on a foreign throne.

Fact 286: Barry Marshall was firmly convinced that not stress but rather Helicobacter pylori bacteria are the main cause of stomach ulcers. In a self-experiment in 1984, he therefore drank a test tube of the bacteria and shortly thereafter developed severe gastritis, which he successfully cured with antibiotics. In 2005, he was awarded the Nobel Prize for his research on Helicobacter pylori together with John Robin Warren.

Fact 287: According to a survey from 2008, about 58 percent of British teens believed that Sherlock Homes really existed.

Fact 288: The world's longest escalator is 453 feet long and located in St. Petersburg, Russia.

Fact 289: When a Fiat employee realized when the Google Street View car will record Södertälje in Sweden, he parked a Fiat in front of the Swedish Volkswagen headquarter to be present in Google Street View for the next years.

Fact 290: The Make-A-Wish-Foundation collects money to fulfil the dreams of seriously ill children.

Fact 291: The spider species "Amaurobius Ferox" belongs to the genus of matriphages. This means that the spider female's children eat their own mother after hatching from their eggs.

Fact 292: "Pikachurin" is a protein that facilitates the correct transmission of electrical signals between the eye and the brain. It was discovered by Japanese scientists and named after the Pokémon Pikachu.

Fact 293: On 24 February 1891, the "United States of Brazil" were founded, and the name of the country lasted for almost 40 years. So at the time, the American continent was home to not only the USA, but also the USB.

Fact 294: In terms of stress levels people aged 18-33 face the hardest challenges.

Fact 295: Walnuts contain just as much protein as eggs.

Fact 296: Wombat excrements are cube-shaped. So far, we have not been able to determine the evolutionary advantage of excreta in this shape. It is assumed, however, that it allows the animals to better mark their territory.

Fact 297: In the U.S. most movies are released on Independence Day. Conversely, the movie "Independence Day" was released a week prior to Independence Day.

Fact 298: In 2015, the Italian city of Collecchio passed a law that only allowed the use of silent fireworks. The objective of this is to reduce stress on animals and children. Since then, many other European cities have followed this example.

Fact 299: On the island of Yap in the western Pacific, the islanders used stone wheels as a monetary unit for centuries. The largest stone wheel had a diameter of 12 feet and weighed more than five tons.

Fact 300: When rebels stormed the home of Muammar al-Gaddafi, they discovered a photo album with pictures of the former U.S. Secretary of State Condoleezza Rice.

Fact 301: Because emus and kangaroos are not able to walk backwards, they are officially referred to as heraldic animals of Australia.

Fact 302: It is unknown where Mozart was buried exactly.

Fact 303: According to the Bible, the chicken came before the egg (Genesis 1:20-22).

Fact 304: On 27 July, Finland celebrates "National Sleepy Head Day". There is a tradition that the last person in a household to wake up in the morning of this day is thrown into a cold lake.

Fact 305: The Soviet Union had its own top-level domain. Until the collapse of the nation, there was a time window of 15 months during which it was possible to register domains with the ending ".su".

Fact 306: The skin that snakes leave behind during moulting is called a "snake shirt".

Fact 307: In Sri Lanka, killing an elephant is punishable by death.

Fact 308: The two great Cuban revolutionaries - Che Guevara and Fidel Castro - both have a doctorate degree. Che was a medical doctor, Fidel a lawyer.

Fact 309: In the USA, there is a sports league for rock-paper-scissors competitions.

Fact 310: At minimum, a person only needs one kidney with a capacity of at least 75 percent to survive.

Fact 311: During the Nuremberg Trials, a psychological test and an intelligence test were carried out on many accused Nazi functionaries and high-ranking military personnel. All Nazi leaders (except for Julius Streicher) displayed above-average intelligence, and some even had an IQ of 140. The former commander of the German Air Force, Hermann Göring, for example, had an IQ of 138.

Fact 312: American school buses are yellow because a study from the 1930s showed that people can perceive the color yellow from a very long distance and therefore the risk of the school buses being involved in accidents decreases.

Fact 313: From 1781 to 1850, the planet Uranus was named George.

Fact 314: Sharks were on the earth before trees existed.

Fact 315: Mel Blanc, who became famous as the voice of Bugs Bunny, was allergic to carrots.

Fact 316: In biological terms, love is an addiction. The serotonin level among lovers is as low as among drug dependents.

Fact 317: The Norwegian Lundehund is the only type of dog with six toes per paw.

Fact 318: The vaginal fluid of women can be found in sharks.

Fact 319: The last time all living human beings were on Earth was on 2 November 2000. Since then, the International Space Station has been continuously occupied.

Fact 320: In 2002, long-distance runner Tom Johnson competed against a horse in an 50-mile race. He ran the distance in five hours and 45 minutes, arriving ten seconds ahead of the horse.

Fact 321: The long drink "gin and tonic" was invented by the British in the 17th century as protection against malaria. The reason for this is that until 1940, the quinine contained in tonic water was the only substance known to be effective against malaria. However, since this also causes the tonic water to taste bitter, the drink was mixed with gin to improve its taste.

Fact 322: In Ukraine there is a 1,000 feet deep salt mine, which is used in the treatment of respiratory diseases. Due to the high salt content, there are fewer bacteria in the air than compared to the most sterile rooms of a hospital.

Fact 323: Around 35 percent of all billionaires have never graduated from a university.

Fact 324: Every year, about four million cats are consumed as delicacies in China.

Fact 325: In the time since Pluto was discovered approximately 75 years ago, it has only traveled one third of its way around the sun.

Fact 326: The largest hydrogen bomb that has been detonated caused such a big shock wave that it could still be measured after the third circumnavigation of the globe.

Fact 327: The human brain needs 33 milliseconds to determine the mood of a person, from their facial expressions alone.

Fact 328: The Candlefish is so oily, that it used to be burned and used as a candle.

Fact 329: In Iowa, a 99 year old senior woman sews one dress every day to donate them to children in Africa.

Fact 330: More than 250,000 millionaires live in New York.

Fact 331: Schwuugle describes itself as "the gay search engine".

Fact 332: With a height of 380.3 feet, the highest tree in the world is the sequoia "Hyperion" in the Redwood National Park in California.

Fact 333: Defenestration is the term used to describe a person falling out of a window.

Fact 334: If you salt a pineapple, it tastes sweeter.

Fact 335: Gray whales exclusively mate in a threesome.

Fact 336: Scorpions can survive up to two years without food.

Fact 337: A study from 2003 came to the conclusion that French people, among all nations, have the most frequent sex.

Fact 338: Even during the night there are rainbows. They are called "moon bows".

Fact 339: At a height of 2,717 feet, the Burj Khalifa is the tallest building in the world. Due to the skyscraper's height, the upper floors of the building can swing back and forth by five feet in strong winds.

Fact 340: NASA claims it will be able to answer the question if we are alone in universe in the next 20 years.

Fact 341: Sunsets on Mars appear in a blue tone.

Fact 342: Golf balls were originally made of wood.

Fact 343: When the historic Plaza Hotel in New York opened its doors in 1907, one night cost $2.50, which by today's standards would be about $64. Today, however, you have to pay more than $1,000 per night.

Fact 344: Most suicides happen on Mondays.

Fact 345: If a stalactite combines with a stalagmite to form a large pillar, this is called a stalagnate.

Fact 346: The Jewish population is only 0.2 percent, yet 20 percent of all Nobel prizes have been awarded to people of the Jewish faith.

Fact 347: The "Sacred Band of Thebes" was a special unit of the Theban army consisting exclusively of homosexual male couples. It was hoped that the soldiers would prove to be more cohesive, as they would try anything to save their partners.

Fact 348: Nutella has a sun protection factor of 9.5.

Fact 349: To date, 43 Germans have won an Oscar and 81 have been awarded the Nobel Prize.

Fact 350: Most serial killers are born in November.

Fact 351: Nutella was invented during World War II, when an Italian soldier mixed chocolate with hazelnut to stretch his food ration.

Fact 352: In December 2013, the dating app Tinder delivered its first match in Antarctica. It was between a scientist and a visitor who were only a 45-minute helicopter flight apart.

Fact 353: If the US state of California were a separate country, it would be the fifth largest economy in the world and thus economically larger than France or Great Britain.

Fact 354: The Huntsman spider (Heteropoda maxima) is the largest spider species in the world. Adult males usually have a span of up to 12 inches. In Australia, a specimen estimated at 15.7 inches was discovered in 2017.

Fact 355: The production cost of one penny is 1.7 cents.

Fact 356: Yellow teeth are more robust than white teeth.

Fact 357: The average depth of our oceans is 12,467 feet. The deepest point, the Mariana Trench, is even approximately 36,201 feet below sea level.

Fact 358: The scientist Charles Darwin married his own cousin in 1839.

Fact 359: From 2015 to 2016, Englishman Ben Smith ran 401 marathons on 401 days to raise money for the victims of bullying. With his "401 Challenge" he set a world record and covered a total of 10,506 miles.

Fact 360: Eminem's mother sued the rapper because he insulted her several times in his songs. She received damages of 1,600 dollars.

Fact 361: The Golden Gate Bridge is made up of so many wire ropes that put together they would circle the earth three times.

Fact 362: Timothy Ray Brown is the first man to be cured from AIDS. In 2007 he received a bone marrow transplant due to his blood cancer. After the treatment, doctors could not detect HIV in his body anymore. To date, nobody knows how this was possible and whether the disease will come back. This phenomena could only be detected on two further people.

Fact 363: The kidnapping of four-year-old Charley Ross in 1874 is considered to be the first kidnapping in the history of the USA to have been widely reported in the media. The girl, who would never be found, was lured by two men with fireworks and sweets. Due to the worldwide interest in this case, children are still advised not to accept sweets from strangers to this day.

Fact 364: Financially, World War I did not end for Germany until 2010, when the last of the reparations payments under the Treaty of Versailles was made.

Fact 365: The "Chewbacca defense" is a term commonly used in the United States for the legal or political defense of a position using nonsensical arguments. The term derives from an episode of the animated series "South Park", in which this defense strategy was used to mock O. J. Simpson's lawyer.

Fact 366: Crickets consist of up to 70 percent protein, while beef steaks contain only 17 to 40 percent protein.

Fact 367: Whittier is a city in Alaska with 217 inhabitants. Almost the entire population of the city lives in the small community's only building, which also houses a school, a hospital, a church and a grocery store. For this, the town has been nicknamed the "town under one roof".

Fact 368: Django Unchained was the first movie in sixteen years in which Leonardo DiCaprio wasn't the highest paid actor on set.

Fact 369: In 1974, North Korea ordered 1,000 Volvo vehicles and other equipment worth 73 million euros from Sweden. To this day, North Korea has not paid for the shipment, and due to accumulated interest the debt has increased to more than 300 million euros.

Fact 370: In its home market of South Korea, Samsung is more than just a tech company. A South Korean can be born in a Samsung-run hospital, live in a Samsung apartment, attend Samsung University and be buried by a Samsung funeral home.

Fact 371: When your fingers swell from being underwater too long, it is because of an evolutionary trait of your nervous system. The fingers swell so as to provide more grip in wet conditions.

Fact 372: In the Brazilian prison of Santa Rita do Sapucaí, inmates can ride stationary bicycles to generate electricity for the city's inhabitants. For every 24 hours of cycling, their detention time is shortened by one day.

Fact 373: A normal person can distinguish up to one million colors. Approximately three percent of the female population can, however, perceive over 100 million different colors due to an additional photoreceptor in the eye.

Fact 374: In 2008, the average age in Uganda was 15. This means that about 50 percent of the population was under the age of 15 at that time.

Fact 375: The heart of a shrimp is located in its head.

Fact 376: The majority of Canada's population lives south of Seattle.

Fact 377: The composition of breast milk adapts to the age and thus to the needs of a child.

Fact 378: Throughout the story of "How I Met Your Mother," there were only twelve incidents in which Barney Stinson did not wear a suit.

Fact 379: In 1647 Christmas was forbidden by the English Parliament.

Fact 380: Sean Connery was wearing a hairpiece for all his James Bond movies because he already began balding at the age of 21.

Fact 381: Born in 1930, Irene Triplett is the last living descendant of a civil war veteran. Although the US civil war ended in 1865, she continues to receive her late father's veteran's pension of $73.13 every month. Her father Mose Triplett was only 18 years old when he went to war and 83 when Irene was born.

Fact 382: The easternmost point of Brazil is closer to Africa than the westernmost point of Brazil.

Fact 383: J. K. Rowling - the author of the Harry Potter books - is no longer a billionaire. She has donated most of her fortune.

Fact 384: A long, thin string is stretched around a part of Manhattan, used by the Jewish population for orientation on the Sabbath.

Fact 385: Genetically, mushrooms are closer to humans than to plants.

Fact 386: Nepal is the only country in the world that does not have a rectangular flag.

Fact 387: Due to earthquakes and tsunamis, Tokyo was destroyed and rebuilt on average every five years between 1608 and 1945.

Fact 388: Genetically, humans possess the requirements for hibernation.

Fact 389: Angola has more Portuguese speaking people than Portugal.

Fact 390: The first hard disk for Apple II had a capacity of five megabyte.

Fact 391: In Brazil, a termite mound was discovered that is probably up to 4,000 years old - almost as old as the pyramids in Egypt.

Fact 392: Black panthers are not an actual species. Instead, these are really leopards or jaguars that due to a genetic defect have a black coat.

Fact 393: On average, a person farts 14 times a day.

Fact 394: In the US state of Illinois, there is a restaurant called "Burger King" that is not part of the fast food chain. Since the restaurant secured the rights to the name earlier, it won the legal dispute with the Burger King chain. To this day, the franchise is not allowed to open a branch within a radius of 20 miles.

Fact 395: NASA has developed a device called "Finder" that can detect a person's breathing and heartbeat even under a 16-feet-thick layer of concrete. It was used to find buried people after the 2015 earthquake in Nepal.

Fact 396: Hippopotami on average kill 2,900 humans per year, stags 130, ants 30, cows 22, horses 20 and sharks only five. But who would run away from a cow?

Fact 397: The cousins of Sailor Moon are Sailor Uranus and Sailor Neptune.

Fact 398: The mad hatter from "Alice in Wonderland" is based on the fact that in the 18th century hatmakers often suffered from mental illnesses. For a long time, people were not sure why this was the case, but then they discovered that the mercury used by hatmakers to make hats caused mental disorders.

Fact 399: In 2006, scientists officially declared that the egg came first, not the chicken.

Fact 400: The average rent for a one room apartment in Manhattan is 3,400 dollars.

Fact 401: The election slogan "Yes we can" actually comes from "Bob the Builder".

Fact 402: Women suffering from "hyperlactation syndrome" produce excessive amounts of breast milk - up to 1.6 gallons of milk a day. A woman's average milk production is usually less than 0.3 gallons per day.

Fact 403: To date, there have been a total of 2,055 atomic bomb tests worldwide. 1,039 were carried out by the USA alone, 718 by the Soviet Union and 198 by France.

Fact 404: If all the gold in the world was melted, a dice with an edge length of 66 feet would be the result.

Fact 405: A "déjà-rêvé" is a dream déjà-vu. So this is a real event of which you believe that you have already seen in a dream.

Fact 406: Cats are the most popular pet in the United States. There are 88 million cats compared to 74 million dogs.

Fact 407: Water cannot go bad and yet there is always an expiration date on water bottles. The reason for this is that the expiration date does not apply to water, but rather indicates when the plastic bottle starts releasing chemicals into the water.

Fact 408: Robert Downey Jr. was the only actor who was allowed to read the entire script of "Avengers: Endgame".

Fact 409: By his 13th birthday, Mike Tyson had already been arrested 38 times.

Fact 410: In 2014 a woman was saved from her burning house. She then realized she had forgot her mobile phone in the house, ran back into her home and died.

Fact 411: Barney Stinson from "How I met your Mother" is the real inventor of the "Bro-Code". Based on Google search analytics the term hadn't existed before 2008.

Fact 412: There is a low probability that women can become pregnant a second time during pregnancy. This so-called phenomenon of "superfetation" is highly unlikely, but nevertheless possible. The last known case of a woman who was pregnant twice at the same time occurred in 2009.

Fact 413: In Clark County, Nevada, there is a house that is an almost exact replica of the Simpson family house.

Fact 414: More people know the logo of McDonald's than the Christian Cross.

Fact 415: During World War II, Queen Elizabeth worked as a mechanic for the British troops.

Fact 416: The weirdest things that have been found in food sold by McDonald's are: bandaging material, the head of a chicken and a dead rat.

Fact 417: Approximately 70 percent of the world's total oxygen is released by plants in the oceans.

Fact 418: Costa Rica does not have its own military anymore. Instead, the money is now spent on education and culture.

Fact 419: During the volcanic eruption of 1902 in Saint-Pierre all inhabitants of the city died. Only one man who was held as a prisoner outside the city survived.

Fact 420: A nap improves your memory and protects against heart disease.

Fact 421: After Steve Jobs' secretary was late due to her car breaking down, he later that afternoon gave her the keys to a new Jaguar, and told her, "Here, don't be late anymore."

Fact 422: Researchers in Australia are working on a new condom made of cellulose that is 30 percent thinner but 20 percent more robust.

Fact 423: Instead of "LOL" people in France say MDR for "mort de rire", which means laughing to death.

Fact 424: Since 1987 Starbucks on average opens two stores a day.

Fact 425: Crows are among the most intelligent non-primates on earth. They possess the intelligence of a toddler, can use tools, have a long-term memory, can recognize faces and understand analogies.

Fact 426: In 2016, in an experiment, a monkey succeeded in moving a wheelchair in which it was sitting through its thoughts alone.

Fact 427: 300 is the film with the most deaths per minute in film history. On average, more than five people die in one minute.

Fact 428: Apple owns more cash than the United States.

Fact 429: In 2005 and 2007, graffiti artist David Choe painted several works of art in Facebook's offices. Instead of cash, however, he was paid with Facebook shares, which were worth over $200 million when the company went public.

Fact 430: Adolf Hitler's nephew William Patrick Hitler emigrated to the USA in 1939 and even fought alongside the Americans against Nazi Germany during the Second World War. He was even awarded the Purple Heart for his accomplishments during the war. After the war, however, he changed his name to William Patrick Stuart-Houston.

Fact 431: Qizai is the name of the only brown panda bear in the world. Its brown coat color is due to a genetic mutation.

Fact 432: Every year, Finland grows by about 2.7 square miles. Due to melting glaciers, the land mass becomes lighter and slowly rises out of the sea.

Fact 433: The shoe size of the Statue of Liberty is size 879.

Fact 434: The dance style "Daggering" was forbidden on Jamaican television, as it lead to numerous penis fractures during the dancing.

Fact 435: As Burger King has no rights to its brand name in Australia, the fast food chain is called "Hungry Jack's" there.

Fact 436: The actor Nicolas Cage has already purchased his own grave. It is a pyramid several meters high in New Orleans.

Fact 437: The urine and sweat of people suffering from "leucinosis" smells of maple syrup. Those affected lack an enzyme needed to break down certain protein elements. For this reason, their bodies increasingly contain the degradation product "sotolone", which smells strongly of maple syrup.

Fact 438: Male ants have no fathers because unfertilized ant eggs always produce male ants and only fertilized eggs produce female ants.

Fact 439: The 1996 Nokia Communicator was the first ever smartphone, it cost 800 dollars and even had a fax connection.

Fact 440: The Swedish man Max Martin is the most successful music composer in the world. Among others he wrote the songs "Wish You Were Here", "Quit Playing Games With My Heart", "I Want You Back", "Oops! ... I Did It Again", "It's My Life", "Since U Been Gone", "I Kissed a Girl", "Hot n Cold", "Dynamite", "DJ Got Us Falling' in Love" and "Fucking Perfect".

Fact 441: When Wilhelm Röntgen discovered a new form of radiation, he could not think of a suitable name for this phenomenon, so he simply called it X-radiation. This is the reason why to this day the rays are called "X rays" in English, while in German-speaking countries they are known as "Röntgen rays".

Fact 442: During World War II, Adolf Hitler gave the order to spare the British city of Blackpool from bomb attacks, as he intended to go on holiday there after Germany had won the war.

Fact 443: Many different bacteria are located in a woman's vagina. Much of those bacteria are also found in yogurt.

Fact 444: Africa is the world's second largest continent. Only Asia is larger.

Fact 445: In India, forest workers wear masks with a picture of a human face on their back of the heads so that they are not attacked by tigers.

Fact 446: According to a social study conducted by Arizona State University, men think they are smarter than equally smart women. Women, on the other hand, tend to underestimate their abilities.

Fact 447: Samsung is responsible for 20 percent of South Korea's gross domestic product.

Fact 448: The maiden name of Goethe's mother was "Textor".

Fact 449: Nowadays, 82 percent of young people do not ring doors anymore, but send a message that they have arrived and wait outside the door.

Fact 450: Flipper was played by five different dolphins.

Fact 451: One side effect of aspirin is headache.

Fact 452: A study concluded that people with a lower IQ more frequently tend to be more homophobic and racist than people with a higher IQ.

Fact 453: In Japan, a woman was sentenced to death in 2017 for killing her three husbands with poison between 2007 and 2012. Previously, she had searched dating portals for wealthy men in order to marry them and then acquire their assets through violent death. She managed to make about 7.7 million euros with this strategy. She therefore became known as the "Black Widow".

Fact 454: Israel is the only country in the world that has seen a net increase in trees over the last 100 years.

Fact 455: The thermometer was invented in Italy.

Fact 456: Taking into account the French overseas regions in the Pacific, Atlantic and Indian Oceans, France is the country with the most time zones. In total, there are twelve different ones.

Fact 457: The domain www.nissan.com belongs to the American Uzi Nissan, who claimed the website for himself back in 1994. He has been in litigation with the car manufacturer Nissan for many years because Uzi Nissan does not want to sell the domain.

Fact 458: Water only gets the typical chlorine smell when someone pees in the basin.

Fact 459: At the US Arlington National Cemetery, there is a group of women who call themselves the "Arlington Ladies". Since their inception in 1948, they have voluntarily committed themselves to attend every funeral ceremony in Arlington so that no soldier needs to be buried alone. On average, the women attend 30 funerals a week.

Fact 460: When Arnold Schwarzenegger wrote a veto letter to the State Assembly of California during his time as Governor of California, it turned out that the first letters of each line formed the word "Fuck You". At first, Schwarzenegger claimed that this was just a coincidence, but in his biography he later confirmed that he had intentionally placed this hidden message.

Fact 461: The original name of the movie "Scream" was "Scary movie".

Fact 462: It is genetically determined whether you can role your tongue or not.

Fact 463: NASA has special wristwatches produced for some of its employees that show the time of day on Mars.

Fact 464: During the nine seasons of "How I Met Your Mother" Ted dated 29 women who were not the mother.

Fact 465: Human gastric acid is so corrosive that it could dissolve a razor blade.

Fact 466: In Newfoundland (Canada) there is a city called Dildo.

Fact 467: If all the ships currently in service in the world were to sink, the sea level would fall minimally and not rise, as one might intuitively think.

Fact 468: In Paris there is only one stop sign.

Fact 469: The role of the character Captain Jack Sparrow from "Pirates of the Caribbean" was originally given to Jim Carry. He refused as he rather wanted to make Bruce Almighty.

Fact 470: In the USA, more money is spent on slot machines than on cinema, baseball and amusement parks combined.

Fact 471: Before McDonald's offered burgers, the company sold hot dogs.

Fact 472: The first successful blood transfusion took place in 1660 and was between two dogs.

Fact 473: Reading reduces your stress level much more than listening to music or walking.

Fact 474: One of the founders of the DNA structure - James Watson - was forced to sell his Nobel Prize in 2014 due to financial problems. He received 4.1 million dollars and the buyer gave him the Nobel Prize back afterwards.

Fact 475: A phenomenon referred to as the "CSI effect" explains when jurymen become influenced by television series such as "CSI Miami".

Fact 476: Cherophobia is the fear of fun.

Fact 477: The word "alphabet" consists of the words "alpha" and "beta", which are the first two letters in the Greek alphabet.

Fact 478: With almost 280,000 visitors, the Frankfurt Book Fair is the largest book fair in the world.

Fact 479: During World War I the Emperor of Germany, the King of Great Britain and the Emperor of Russia were all first cousins. The German Emperor Wilhelm II therefore commented sarcastically on the First World War: "If our grandmother (Queen Victoria) were still alive, she would never have allowed it."

Fact 480: The term "bug" for a programing error dates back to the 19th century. At the time, engineers were afraid that small bugs could destroy transmissions and cause malfunctions. When the computer was later invented, there were indeed several incidents in which insects caused a system to crash. With that, the term "bug" stuck once and for all.

Fact 481: Jack Daniel's now also sells whiskey-flavored coffee beans.

Fact 482: After a 19 year old girl became the three millionth follower of Venezuelan President Hugo Chávez on Facebook, the president gave her a house.

Fact 483: The first part of the horror film series "Paranormal Activity" only had a production budget of 15,000 dollars, but went on to take in over 194 million dollars at the box office.

Fact 484: Thioacetone is considered the world's worst smelling chemical. According to reports, when parts of the substance were released from a production site in Freiburg in 1889, it was reported that within a radius of 2,460 feet passers-by suddenly had to vomit because of the unbearable smell.

Fact 485: At a wedding ceremony, women usually stand to the left of the groom. This has historical reasons, as this way the man's sword hand was free to protect the woman from any attackers.

Fact 486: The world record for the most consecutive push-ups was set in 1980 by Minoru Yoshida from Japan who managed to do 10,507 in a row.

Fact 487: The Vatican has its own telephone company, its own radio station, its own TV station, its own stamps, its own currency and its own army.

Fact 488: The Titanoboa was the largest snake to ever have lived. The 46-foot-long animal, which weighed more than 1.3 tons, haunted the Colombian rainforest some 60 million years ago.

Fact 489: The release of the film "The Princess and the Frog" led to more than 50 cases in the US where children were infected with a disease because they had kissed a frog.

Fact 490: In Lazio (Italy) policemen drive Lamborghinis.

Fact 491: During the production of "Toy Story 2", an employee accidentally erased the whole movie and almost ruined the production. Fortunately, one of the employees had a backup on her desktop computer, so the work went on and the movie made it to the cinemas.

Fact 492: The Paricutín volcano in Mexico was not there until 20 February 1943. Witnesses report having worked on a maize field that day and heard a dull "plop". A day later, the volcano was already 33 feet high, and by the next day it had grown to 164 feet. A year later, the volcano had reached a height of 1,102 feet when it began to spew lava. Today, the volcano is 1,391 feet high and continues to be active.

Fact 493: Bob Marley's song "No Woman No Cry" was actually called "No Woman Nuh Cry". This song is not about the better life of men without women, but about the life of a sad woman.

Fact 494: There is a woman whose name is actually "Marijuana Pepsi Jackson". The African-American woman now carries the surname Vandyck and wrote her dissertation on unusual black names in the classroom.

Fact 495: The gigantism of the dinosaurs and many other prehistoric animal species can be traced back to epochs with a significantly increased oxygen concentration in the air. For example, the oxygen content in the Carboniferous was 35 percent instead of the current 21 percent.

Fact 496: In France there is a village named "Pussy".

Fact 497: A study came to the conclusion that the lack of exercise in the Western world kills the same amount of people as smoking does.

Fact 498: Only two percent of all people have green eyes.

Fact 499: When California was exposed to an extreme drought in 1915, a "rainmaker" was hired by the City of San Diego and promised a payment of 10,000 dollars if he managed to summon rain. Shortly thereafter it rained for almost a month without interruption, resulting in numerous floods and destroyed dams. The city council decided that this must have been a sign from God, so they did not pay the rainmaker.

Fact 500: When it comes to extreme heat in Melbourne, the lions in the zoo are given frozen blood.

Fact 501: In 2009, a ten year old tried to sell his grandma on eBay.

Fact 502: One of the original ingredients of Coca-Cola was cocaine

Fact 503: In 1997, Microsoft employed 31,000 people worldwide, of which 21,000 already were millionaires because of their participation in the company.

Fact 504: An anonymous donor pays for the college tuition of each student in Kalamazoo, Michigan.

Fact 505: The word "blood" is mentioned at least once in every Shakespeare piece.

Fact 506: If 57 people are gathered in one room, the likelihood of two of the people having their birthday on the same day, is about 99 percent.

Fact 507: The Russian Fyodor Vasilyev holds the record for most children fathered by a man with a woman. In the 18th century, his wife gave birth to a total of 69 children, including four sets of quadruplets, seven sets of triplets and 16 pairs of twins. Later on, he married again and fathered another 18 children with his second wife, including two sets of triplets and six pairs of twins.

Fact 508: In Finland, there are more saunas than cars. There are a total of 2.2 million saunas for 5.4 million inhabitants.

Fact 509: Will Smith was originally supposed to play the role of Neo in "Matrix". However, he refused and preferred to do "Wild Wild West" instead.

Fact 510: Diabetic patients are unable to regulate their blood glucose level. For this reason, the glucose level is sometimes so high that even the urine of a diabetic patient would taste sweet.

Fact 511: Bangladesh, although just one percent the size of Russia, is more populated.

Fact 512: In 1995, Newsweek published an article in which it expressed the opinion that the Internet would never make it. Meanwhile, this article is available on their website.

Fact 513: "Almost" is the longest word in the English language in which all letters are arranged in alphabetical order.

Fact 514: For his first role in Star Wars Episode 4, Han Solo actor Harrison Ford received $10,000 in 1977, while for Episode 7 in 2015 he was paid $20 million.

Fact 515: If you start counting from one, then 1,000 is the first number in which the letter "A" occurs.

Fact 516: Male reindeer shed their antlers every year at Christmas time. However, since Santa's reindeer all have antlers, they must be either female or neutered.

Fact 517: McDonald's is not the largest restaurant chain in the world. Subway is.

Fact 518: Bulletproof glass can be made in such a way that it is bulletproof only from one side and allows bullets to pass through from the other.

Fact 519: The superhero "The Access" belongs to both DC and Marvel. He has the ability to open an inter-dimensional gate between both comic worlds.

Fact 520: Jonah Falcon has the biggest penis in the world. It has a length of almost 14 inches.

Fact 521: YouTube Blocked in Tajikistan After a Video of the President Dancing Goes Viral.

Fact 522: In 2011, torero Juan José Padilla lost his left eye during a bullfight. Five years later, the one-eyed bullfighter was once again caught by a bull - in the same spot.

Fact 523: Penguins can jump six feet high.

Fact 524: All faces we see in our dreams are faces of people we have already met in real life.

Fact 525: "The Pineapple Incident" is the most watched episode of "How I Met Your Mother".

Fact 526: Around 75 percent of all vehicles, which were produced by Rolls-Royce, are still in operation.

Fact 527: A short nap after studying helps the brain to remember the studied materials better.

Fact 528: If you feel very connected to a person, you can hear their voice in your head when you read messages they have sent.

Fact 529: In the U.S., the probability of suicide is twice the rate of an assassination by a third party.

Fact 530: The likelihood of getting bitten by a human in New York is higher than the likelihood of getting bitten by a shark in the sea.

Fact 531: When Saudi King Salman travels in his private jet, he always takes a golden escalator along to exit the plane.

Fact 532: When the height of Mount Everest was first determined in the 19th century, researchers calculated a total height of exactly 29,000 feet. The height they published, however, was 29,002 feet, as the researchers feared that a figure as even as 29,000 feet might be interpreted as a rough estimate.

Fact 533: According to FIFA, the five meter space of a football field must be 5.50 meters wide.

Fact 534: To keep up with speedsters, the police of Dubai are equipped with Ferraris and Lamborghinis.

Fact 535: Although women's brains are slightly smaller, they are more efficient than men's brains.

Fact 536: An iPad with apps installed weighs more than an iPad without apps installed.

Fact 537: If you write "3:)" on Facebook you will see a little surprise.

Fact 538: In Stockholm Sweden, there is a pilot project, which involves receiving an SMS when someone has a heart attack nearby and the ambulance has been called. Then the receiver can rush to the location and execute a heart lung massage. So far 9,500 people have joined this project and in 54 percent of the cases, people reach the location before the ambulance and were able to provide assistance.

Fact 539: During "How I Met Your Mother" there have been 13 interventions. The most popular ones were Barneys frequent usage of magic tricks, Marshals addiction to charts and Lilly's fake British accent.

Fact 540: The entire border between the United States and Canada consists of a cleared strip of forest with a width of approximately 20 feet.

Fact 541: In Greece, there are over 2,000 people who have registered as officially practicing the religion "Hellenism". This means that they believe in the ancient Greek gods like Zeus, Poseidon or Aphrodite.

Fact 542: Bill Gates has already donated more than 28 billion dollars since 2007. It is estimated that this has saved about six million lives.

Fact 543: The "dingo fence" is a fence in Australia designed to protect sheep in the southeast of the continent from predators. It has a total length of 3,363 miles.

Fact 544: Burger King offers free burgers for life to celebrities who want to promote their fast food.

Fact 545: The name "Microsoft" is a combination of "microcomputer" and "software".

Fact 546: Renfield-Syndrome is characterized by an obsession with drinking blood.

Fact 547: Since 1944, Iceland does not have its own army, and have not been attacked by other countries since.

Fact 548: The oxygen levels of a fetus in the womb are almost as low as on Mount Everest. The low oxygen level helps the fetus to sleep most of its time in the womb.

Fact 549: Before coffee became popular, beer was served for breakfast in the USA.

Fact 550: Leonardo da Vinci loved animals so much that he often bought caged animals to set them free.

Fact 551: Ruby Bridges was the first black child to attend a whites-only school in the southern United States. Most of the teachers at the New Orleans school refused to teach the girl, and some parents forbid their children to make contact with their new schoolmate. Ruby and her family received death threats over and over again, so she initially had to be escorted to school by at least three police officers.

Fact 552: The human heartbeat changes when listening to music and adapts to the sound.

Fact 553: The human circadian rhythm is better suited to life on Mars than on Earth.

Fact 554: People with blue eyes have a higher tolerance threshold for alcohol and are therefore drunk only after consuming larger quantities of alcohol.

Fact 555: Cats sweat through their paws.

Fact 556: Monopoly was developed in 1930 in the U.S. to create a pastime for the unemployed people during the great depression.

Fact 557: A "kakistocracy" is a system of government where a country is ruled by the worst and least qualified persons.

Fact 558: Because a big butt is a sign of fertility, men feel more attracted to women with larger butts.

Fact 559: Fully-grown bears can run as fast as horses.

Fact 560: Sneezing too intensively can cause a broken rib.

Fact 561: About 80 percent of people breathe exclusively through one nostril. Which nostril is used by the body varies approximately every 2.5 hours. While the other nostril is not being used for breathing, the body cleans it.

Fact 562: One pound of muscles burns 16,300 calories per year.

Fact 563: In Korea, everyone is one year old from birth and turns one year older on New Year's Day.

Fact 564: More than 50 percent of the world's population has never received a phone call.

Fact 565: Kizhi Pogost is a church in Russia which was built more than 300 years ago and is made exclusively from wood. It is over 115 feet high and does not contain a single nail.

Fact 566: If you could power an iPhone with gasoline, one drop would be enough to use the smartphone for a whole day.

Fact 567: Thanks to a language computer, Stephen Hawking could speak at a rate of one word per minute.

Fact 568: The "Jesus nut" is the bolt that holds the rotor blades of a helicopter together. The name of the bolt was given by its importance. When it breaks, only a prayer to Jesus helps one to survive.

Fact 569: The least people are born in February.

Fact 570: One fifth of all people use their smartphone during sex.

Fact 571: With a total length of about 4,132 miles (6,650 kilometres) the Nile River is the longest river in the world.

Fact 572: Eggs can explode in the microwave.

Fact 573: With more than 500 kills, the Finnish soldier Simo Häyhä is the sniper with the highest number of confirmed kills in a war. He fought during the Second World War and killed mainly Soviet soldiers. The Red Army called him "The White Death".

Fact 574: Regular sex can relieve nasal congestion and help treat asthma and hay fever.

Fact 575: The anchor motif as a tattoo was originally meant to signal that the carrier had already crossed the Atlantic.

Fact 576: During the first days in space, astronauts often suffer from space sickness. Since all bodily fluids are redistributed in weightlessness and the sense of balance is impaired, important tasks such as outboard work are not carried out in the first days of a space mission. There would be an acute risk of the astronauts throwing up in their suits.

Fact 577: 32-year-old Wombat "Patrick" living in Australia was the oldest animal of his species. As he was not able to find a female partner, his keepers even created a Tinder profile for him.

Fact 578: Scientists believe they have discovered an evolutionary jump. It was discovered that the Australian lizard stems from an egg-laying species to a viviparous one.

Fact 579: Four out of five people sing in the car.

Fact 580: The vampire bat has an enzyme that prevents its victims' blood from clotting on wounds. As a result, the victims lose more blood that the vampire bats can then feed on.

Fact 581: In 2005 a used pregnancy test belonging to Britney Spears was sold for more than 5,000 dollars on Ebay.

Fact 582: During the 1904 Summer Olympics in St. Louis, the American Frederick Lorz was the first to reach the finish line of the marathon race. It turned out, however, that he had covered about half the distance by car.

Fact 583: While the mortality rate for cancer ten years ago was 215 deaths per 100,000 people, it has subsequently decreased to 172.

Fact 584: It is estimated that there are more than 270 million fake accounts on Facebook.

Fact 585: Australian rower Bobby Pearce won the 1928 Olympic Games against eight other competitors, even though he stopped during the race to let ducks pass in front of him.

Fact 586: Each year a lying competition takes place in England. Participants have to tell a made up story for five minutes. To be "fair", politicians and lawyers are not allowed to participate.

Fact 587: A building on the Amazon campus - the Wainwright Building - was named after the website's first customer.

Fact 588: It only takes one drop of engine oil to contaminate more than 25 liters of water.

Fact 589: In the fun sport Headis, two players compete against each other following the rules of table tennis. However, the game is played with a special ball the size of a football, which may only be touched with the head. In 2017 the twelfth Headis World Championships were held.

Fact 590: Mangalica pigs are a rare type of pig that due to their curly, light bristles look like sheep.

Fact 591: The founder of Wikipedia - Jimmy Wales - has only a fortune of about one million dollars.

Fact 592: In Finland, Valentine's Day is called Ystävänpäivä ("Friends' Day"). So there, the day is not only dedicated to one's partner, but also to one's circle of friends.

Fact 593: Babies can already get an erection in the womb.

Fact 594: Up until his death, F. Scott Fitzgerald was convinced that he had achieved nothing in his life. Two years later, his book "The Great Gatsby" was sent to soldiers in World War II and became an immediate success. To this day, the book sells about 500,000 copies every year.

Fact 595: All of our school textbooks show the solar system with the planets close enough to fit on one page. In actuality if you were to draw the solar system to scale and the earth was the size of a pea on paper Jupiter would be over 984 feet away and Pluto would be one and a half mile away. The nearest star would be 9,940 miles away on paper.

Fact 596: Mexican priest Sergio Gutiérrez Benítez supported an orphanage for over 23 years by earning money as a wrestler under the pseudonym "Fray Tormenta". He became known all over the world for his distinctive mask, which he now wears even during his sermons in church.

Fact 597: Algerian hacker Hamza Bendelladj stole 280 million dollars from over 200 banks and donated most of the money to aid organizations in Palestine. In 2015, he was sentenced to 30 years in prison in the United States.

Fact 598: At a height of almost 12 miles and above the air pressure is so low, that water in your body would vaporize due your own body temperature.

Fact 599: A few hours after an infection with HIV, post-exposure prophylaxis which can significantly reduce the risk of contracting the virus is possible.

Fact 600: 60% of the African continent is covered by deserts and drylands.

Fact 601: Almost 40% of all adults on Africa are illiterate.

Fact 602: Brryan Jackson's father infected his son with HIV at the age of eleven months to kill him, because he didn't want to pay alimony. Within 5 years the doctors diagnosed AIDS in Jackson. They gave him just a few months. Today, Brryan Jackson is 20 years old and HIV has not been detected in his blood for more than five years.

Fact 603: In North Korea, basketball is played according to different rules. For example, the team loses points if it doesn't score on free throws and a dunk scores three points instead of the usual two.

Fact 604: The average starting salary for a developer at Microsoft is 106,000 dollars.

Fact 605: If. There. Is. A. Period. After. Every. Word. Our. Brain. Automatically. Starts. Making. Pauses. After. Each. Word.

Fact 606: On the occasion of the new Star Wars Movie "The Force Awakens" the weirdest products were sold under the "Star Wars" trade mark. Including a knife block, oranges, mascara and special "Yoda water".

Fact 607: For fun, a British couple invited the Queen to their wedding. The Queen actually came to the wedding.

Fact 608: Dallol is an area in Northern Ethiopia and has the highest average temperature on Earth. The average temperature is 93 degrees Fahrenheit (34 degrees Celsius).

Fact 609: Russian man, Valery Spiridonov was alleged to be the first human to receive a head transplant. His head was to be transplanted to a new body, but he decided against it after a long hesitation. Meanwhile, a Chinese man that hasn't been named is to take his place.

Fact 610: Before the actor James Franco became successful, he practiced different accents while working as a cashier at McDonald's to see his customers reactions.

Fact 611: Over a billion people still have no access to electricity.

Fact 612: It is impossible to sneeze with your eyes open.

Fact 613: The first Subway restaurant was opened in 1965 by a 17-year-old high school graduate looking for a way to finance his tuition fees.

Fact 614: The "Medical Students Disease" describes the phenomenon of medical students suffering from the disease they recently have learned about in class.

Fact 615: French was the national language of Great Britain for more than 300 years.

Fact 616: Iceland has the lowest population density in the EU - only 9.1 people per square mile.

Fact 617: The city with the longest name in the world is Llanfairpwllgwyngyllgogerychwyrndrobwllllantysiliogogog och and is located in Wales.

Fact 618: When the Mona Lisa was stolen from the Louvre in 1911, Pablo Picasso was one of the suspects.

Fact 619: Washing your hands regularly with soap and water is a sufficiently protective mechanism against the Ebola virus.

Fact 620: Pigs cannot see to the sky.

Fact 621: Like humans, ducks have different accents.

Fact 622: According to current estimates, it would cost more than 23 billion dollars to build a real "Jurassic Park".

Fact 623: Jakarta is the fastest sinking city in the world. Every year, the ground sinks by up to ten inches.

Fact 624: On its website, Netflix offers the opportunity to request series or films to be included in the company's online catalogue.

Fact 625: Dolphins sleep with there eyes open.

Fact 626: The guitarist of the rock band Queen has a doctorate in astrophysics.

Fact 627: A red hair color paired with blue eyes is the rarest combination of hair and eye color. Only one percent of the world's population has these characteristics.

Fact 628: "Mr. Bean" actor Rowan Atkinson holds a master's degree in electrical engineering.

Fact 629: An estimated five million landmines are still buried in India.

Fact 630: When the moon is furthest away from Earth, both celestial bodies are so far apart that all the planets in our solar system could fit in between.

Fact 631: If you listen to The Proclaimer's song "I'm Gonna be (500 miles)" while on board on the international space station, you will have travelled approximately 1,000 miles or "500 miles and 500 more".

Fact 632: During World War II, the Nazis attempted to cover the river Alster as part of their "Operation Cloak of Invisibility". They covered parts of the river with wood and wire, built dummy houses and planted trees on the frozen river, as they suspected that the Allies were using the Alster for orientation. The objective was to save Hamburg's city center from more severe bomb damage. However, this hope was not fulfilled.

Fact 633: Although Cape Town is the southernmost city in Africa its not the southernmost point in the continent. That's Cape Agulhas which is roughly 100 miles (170km) southeast from Cape Town.

Fact 634: With one pencil, one is able to draw a line with a length of up to 37 miles.

Fact 635: In 1724 Maggie Dickson from Scotland was sentenced to death by hanging. After she had been hanged and taken away in a coffin, it turned out that she had survived. A court ruled that the sentence was officially carried out, so she could not be punished any further. She continued to live for over 40 years and was nicknamed "Half-Hangit Maggie".

Fact 636: The Twitter account @everyword has tweeted every single word of the English language.

Fact 637: The James Randi Educational Foundation gives one million dollars to any person who can prove, under scientific conditions, that they have paranormal abilities. To this day, no one has received the money.

Fact 638: There is a type of jellyfish which is immortal.

Fact 639: During World War II, the Allies estimated the production rate of German tanks by comparing the serial numbers on captured tanks. The production rate of tanks was estimated at 256 units per month. After the end of the war, the actual production rate was discovered: 255 tanks per month.

Fact 640: After Christmas, Halloween is the holiday generating the highest sales revenues in the United States.

Fact 641: In the United States at least one person per hour gets killed in a car accident due to drinking.

Fact 642: Andorra does not have an army of its own. Instead, the law stipulates that at least every male head of household must possess a weapon for defense purposes. The law even obliges the police to make a weapon available to every male citizen who does not have one.

Fact 643: The Japanese word "karate" means "empty hand".

Fact 644: The former U.S. politician Thomas Jefferson believed that every law should automatically become void after 19 years, to be replaced by a new law, which is adjusted to the new generation.

Fact 645: In the Arabic versions of the cult show, Homer Simpson drinks water instead of beer.

Fact 646: Hawaii plans to pass a law by 2024 prohibiting anyone under the age of 100 from smoking cigarettes.

Fact 647: If one donates a part of one's liver, the missing part will grow again.

Fact 648: The IKEA catalogue is the only book on earth, of which there are more copies than the Bible.

Fact 649: The first person shooter "Half Life" has already been successfully used in the treatment of arachnophobia (the fear of spiders).

Fact 650: The Diomedes Islands are a group of islands in the Arctic Ocean. The western island of this group belongs to Russia, while the eastern island belongs to the USA. Both islands are only 2.5 miles apart, but as the International Date Line runs between them, they are separated by a 21-hour time difference.

Fact 651: Bushes and clouds in Super Mario Bros have the same shape, only the color is different.

Fact 652: The explosion of a modern nuclear atomic bomb in London would produce such a large pressure wave that glass panes in Berlin would also shatter.

Fact 653: If the sum of all the digits of a number is divisible by three, then the number itself can also be divided by three.

Fact 654: Over 50% of the African population is under the age of 25.

Fact 655: In Japan, there is a road system where music is played when a car drives at the right speed.

Fact 656: The designer Ko Yang has invented a milk package that changes its color when the milk begins to spoil.

Fact 657: At Christmas, the number of hits on divorce websites doubles.

Fact 658: A human could survive two minutes in space without a space suit.

Fact 659: Actor Robert Downey Jr. credits Burger King with saving his life. When he wanted to eat a burger from the fast food chain in 2003, he found it so bad that he began rethinking his entire life and decided to put an end to his drug addiction. Five years later, he received the role of Iron Man.

Fact 660: From January 1st to December 31st of 1881, three different men - Rutherford B. Hayes, James A. Garfield and Chester A. Arthur - held the office of President of the United States.

Fact 661: It is assumed that so far only four percent of our oceans have been explored.

Fact 662: Scientists assume that the face of the Sphinx was painted red.

Fact 663: In the 20th century, there were still stomach-breeding frogs living in Australia. The tadpoles grew up in the mother's stomach and climbed out of her mouth as soon as they were big enough.

Fact 664: Contraceptive pills also work for gorillas.

Fact 665: In Kenya, elephant droppings are used to make paper. 110 pounds of excrement can be used to produce 125 pages of paper. The proceeds from the sale of the paper are used to expand the elephant reserve.

Fact 666: Family Guy is the first television series which, after being cancelled, came back to TV, because the DVD sales were so high.

Fact 667: From 1789 to 1790, New York was the capital of the USA.

Fact 668: In 2012, a new ant species was discovered in New York City. Scientists named it "ManhattAnt".

Fact 669: Karaoke is Japanese and means "empty orchestra".

Fact 670: The only Spanish speaking country in Africa is Equatorial Guinea.

Fact 671: Frederic Baur developed the boxing of Pringles Chips. After his death in 2008, his ashes were buried in a Pringles box.

Fact 672: At 386 billion dollars, Austria's gross domestic product in 2016 was lower than the US retail company Walmart's sales revenues for the same year, which was 100 billion dollars higher.

Fact 673: The fast food chain Subway has over 41,000 restaurants. This means that on average, two restaurants have been opened per day since its establishment in 1965.

Fact 674: Canada has more lakes than any other country in the world.

Fact 675: Animals like the zebra, gorilla, giraffe, chimpanzee, wildebeest or hippopotamus are unique to the African continent and can only be found here.

Fact 676: Malaria was once used to treat syphilis. As early as 1917, the Austrian physician Julius Wagner-Jauregg injected syphilis patients with the malaria pathogen in order for the resulting fever to kill the syphilis pathogens. The method of treatment was so successful that Julius Wagner-Jauregg was awarded the Nobel Prize for Medicine in 1927. Since the discovery of penicillin, however, this method of treatment has been abandoned.

Fact 677: 90 percent of all people live in the northern hemisphere.

Fact 678: Leonardo DiCaprio was named after Leonardo da Vinci. His mother was looking at a drawing by the artist in a museum, when she felt young Leonardo move for the first time.

Fact 679: The Romanian scientist Nicolas Minovici explored death by hanging and for his studies hanged himself from a gallows several times.

Fact 680: Being in love releases the same hormones that the use of cocaine releases.

Fact 681: In Spain there is a comedy club in which you pay per laugh.

Fact 682: In France it is not prohibited to marry a dead person.

Fact 683: According to current estimates, there are only three living Northern white rhinos left. So the species is on the verge of extinction.

Fact 684: Throughout its career, the British rock band Pink Floyd has released so many songs with astronomical allusions that scientists have named an asteroid after the band. "19367 Pink Floyd" was discovered in 1997 and has a diameter of over 4,100 miles.

Fact 685: September was originally the seventh month of the year. The name comes from the Latin word "septem", which means "seven".

Fact 686: Dalmatian puppies are born with a white coat. The black dots only appear after a while in the course of their childhood.

Fact 687: Although Japan has only one third of the population of the United States, more than six times as many Japanese people are more than 100 years old.

Fact 688: Amazon was originally supposed to be called "Cadabra". But when the founder's lawyer understood "cadaver", a different name was chosen.

Fact 689: The brain of an ostrich is smaller than its eyes.

Fact 690: David Hasselhoff secured the rights to his nickname "The Hoff" and the phrase "Do not Hassel the Hoff" as part of his divorce settlement.

Fact 691: In Australia, a hog stole 18 beers from a camping site, got drunk and then tried to attack a cow.

Fact 692: Popcorn became a popular cinema snack in the United States during the global economic crisis because it was so cheap.

Fact 693: In a guidebook for spies, the US intelligence agency CIA explained how during the Cold War spies could exchange information using their shoelaces. The message communicated differed depending on how the shoelaces were tied.

Fact 694: In 2013, scientists added human brain cells to a mouse, and it actually went on to demonstrate improved cognitive abilities.

Fact 695: Jessica Cox was born without arms and in 2008 became the first person with this disability to be officially licensed as a pilot. In addition to this, she is also a Taekwondo black belt.

Fact 696: The "Fallen Astronaut Sculpture" is the only work of art on the moon so far. It was created by Belgian artist Paul Van Hoeydonck and brought to the moon during the Apollo 15 mission in 1971. It commemorates the 14 astronauts who died prior to the Apollo 15 mission.

Fact 697: In a kidney transplant, the non-functional kidney is usually not removed from the body. Instead, the new donor kidney is inserted into the groin, meaning that after a kidney transplant, the patient has three kidneys.

Fact 698: During the First World War, a unique event took place on the western front. On Christmas Eve, allied troops stopped their fighting and started singing Christmas carols. The Germans responded by shouting "Merry Christmas". Some of the English then came out of their trenches and ran to the Germans to greet them and shake hands, and then the soldiers even exchanged cigarettes.

Fact 699: To protect the German soldiers from the British night vision technology, they spread the lie that eating lots of carrots helped British soldiers to increase their eyesight during night. A myth was born.

Fact 700: In England, the second Day of Christmas is called "Boxing Day" because employees and servants traditionally received a gift box - the so-called Christmas Box - from their employer.

Fact 701: In the early 50s a "Blow Job" described the bang when breaking the sound barrier.

Fact 702: In 2005, Mark Zuckerberg offered Facebook for 75 million dollars to MySpace. The CEO of MySpace, Chris DeWolfe - declined.

Fact 703: When the Big Bang theory was presented for the first time, it was rejected by many scientists because it seemed too religious.

Fact 704: The first digital camera was invented back in 1975 by a Kodak employee. However, the company dropped the idea as it was assumed that it would negatively impact the sale of film rolls.

Fact 705: It is estimated that 7,000 people die every year because the handwriting of the treating doctor was not legible.

Fact 706: Brazilian natives used ants as wound clamps. They let the ants bite and close the wound with their pincers and then pulled off their bodies. The pincers remained wedged in the body, closing the wound.

Fact 707: Big Ben is only the name of the main bell in the belfry of London. The correct name of the bell tower is "Clock Tower".

Fact 708: The glass globe above the German Reichstag building symbolizes that politics should always be transparent and that the people stand over the government.

Fact 709: Google co-founders Sergey Brin and Larry Page originally named Google "Backrub". It was released in August 1996 and renamed to "Google" in 1997.

Fact 710: With a diameter of up to 6.6 feet and a length of up to 120 feet, the lion's mane jellyfish is the largest jellyfish in the world. It is even longer than a blue whale.

Fact 711: There are more people with obesity than malnutrition worldwide.

Fact 712: Bulls cannot see the color red at all.

Fact 713: At the beginning of the 20th century, radium was often used as an ingredient in facial cream.

Fact 714: The name "Lego" is derived from "Leg Godt", which means "play well" in Danish.

Fact 715: When two wolves mate, they stay together for the rest of their lives.

Fact 716: It is estimated that about 220,000 marriage proposals are made each year on Valentine's Day.

Fact 717: Adrian Carton de Wiart fought in both World Wars and he was shot in his head, his leg, his hips and his ear. He also survived a plane crash and when the doctors were unwilling to amputate two of his fingers, he bit them off. When he was later asked about his time during the war he replied "I had enjoyed the war".

Fact 718: The most common zodiac sign among billionaires is Aquarius. The least common one is Cancer.

Fact 719: When leaving school, a child in the U.S. has already witnessed 40,000 people dying on TV.

Fact 720: Each year about 100 million bikes are produced worldwide.

Fact 721: 66 million years ago, an asteroid with a diameter of 6.2 to 9.3 miles hit the Yucatan peninsula - at the time still a shallow sea. The Chicxulub impact had a force of at least 200 million Hiroshima bombs and directly and indirectly caused the extinction of up to 75 percent of all plant and animal species living at that time.

Fact 722: In 1994, Microsoft, in collaboration with Timex, introduced the world's first smart watch. At that time, however, nobody was interested in it, so production was discontinued.

Fact 723: E.T. was originally a horror movie, in which aliens reach the earth and kill humans by touching their heads with their fingers.

Fact 724: Asia has a larger surface area than the moon. While the surface of the moon measures only 14,645,698 square miles, Asia covers a total of 17,212,368 square miles.

Fact 725: The construction of the Titanic cost seven million dollars. The film starring Leonardo DiCaprio cost 200 million dollars to produce.

Fact 726: During a press conference in the 70's a reporter asked Stevie Wonder, what it was like being born blind. He answered "It could have been worse. I could have been born black."

Fact 727: In preparation of the movie "Rocky" Sylvester Stallone asked the former professional boxer Earnie Shavers to beat him multiple times in the face at full force. Stallone vomited after his first punch.

Fact 728: Monowi in Nebraska has only one inhabitant and he is also mayor of the city.

Fact 729: Falling asleep next to a loved one helps one to doze off faster and decreases the risk of depression.

Fact 730: The American pygmy shrew has to eat three times its own body weight every day. For this, the animal has to go hunting again every 15 to 30 minutes, as even an hour without food would lead to its death.

Fact 731: Queen Elizabeth uses her handbag to send secret signals to her employees. Changing the bag from one hand to the other, for example, constitutes a request to end the current conversation.

Fact 732: With an estimated length of 221 feet, the Patagotitan mayorum was probably the longest dinosaur in the world. Weighing in at about 77 tons, it was as heavy as a Boeing 747 and therefore probably the heaviest land creature of all time.

Fact 733: Africa is only the world's second driest continent. Australia is drier.

Fact 734: The combination of a knife with a fork and a spoon is called spork.

Fact 735: The word "idiot" is a psychology term that describes people with an IQ between 0 and 25.

Fact 736: In India there are milkshakes with marijuana.

Fact 737: Spending more than 15,000 dollars for a wedding increases the rate of divorce compared to couples who have a cheaper wedding.

Fact 738: The teeth of limpets are the hardest biological material in the world.

Fact 739: The US presidential limousine "The Beast" even contains blood reserves in the president's blood type.

Fact 740: The Scottish kilt originally came from France.

Fact 741: When Einstein heard of the book "100 Authors Against Albert Einstein," he replied, "Why 100? If I were wrong, one would be enough."

Fact 742: Until the 1960s, pregnancy tests were carried out by injecting a frog with the test person's urine. If the frog spawned within 12 to 24 hours, it could be assumed that the test person was pregnant.

Fact 743: In 1893, a U.S. citizen made an application to change the name of the country to "The United States of the Earth".

Fact 744: Kit Kat is very popular in Japan. The Japanese expression "Kitto Katsu" loosely translates as "safe profit", which has led to Japanese people often giving away a Kit Kat to wish someone luck.

Fact 745: While the British royal system allows women who marry into the royal family to become queens, men who marry into the royal family cannot become kings. Men who marry into the family only receive the royal title "Prince". This is the reason why the husband of the reigning Queen Elizabeth is only Prince and not King of the United Kingdom.

Fact 746: It takes about 100,000 years for the sun's energy to penetrate out from the core of the sun to the outermost layer and only eight minutes until it reaches the earth.

Fact 747: The suicide rate in Japan is 60 percent above the global average. This is why workshops teaching people to express their feelings are becoming more and more popular in the country.

Fact 748: A 20 second hug increases the oxytocin level of people so much that afterwards there is a much greater trust between them.

Fact 749: The author J. K. Rowling was the first person in the world who became a billionaire by selling books.

Fact 750: On January 1 1985, the first phone call was made using a cellular phone.

Fact 751: The mouthwash "Listerine" was originally marketed as a clinical antiseptic and later, in distilled form, as a floor cleaner.

Fact 752: Because of pressure balance it is impossible to whistle in a space suit.

Fact 753: Short female car drivers have the highest likelihood of being killed by the cars airbag due to their close distance to the steering wheel.

Fact 754: In 1913, Adolf Hitler, Joseph Stalin, Leo Trotsky, and Sigmund Freud all lived close to each other in the immediate vicinity of Vienna, and regularly went to the same cafe without ever having come into contact with each other.

Fact 755: In Amazon's early days, there was a programming error that caused Amazon to pay money to its customers. All you had to do was buy a negative number of books, and the amount was credited to your credit card.

Fact 756: While the Atlantic grows by a few inches every year, the Pacific Ocean is shrinking.

Fact 757: When Great Britain returned Hong Kong to China in 1997 after years of colonization, it was agreed that Hong Kong should continue as a democratic state with its own laws, its own economy and its own currency. However, this agreement will expire in 2047 and China will take full control of Hong Kong from then on.

Fact 758: Based on current extrapolations Bill Gates could be the first trillionaire in the world.

Fact 759: Seen chronologically, Cleopatra was closer to the moon landing than to the construction of the pyramids.

Fact 760: Gnats are especially attracted by people with blood type O.

Fact 761: During the shooting of "The Wolf of Wall Street", actor Jonah Hill had to receive medical treatment after contracting bronchitis due to the excessive intake of fake cocaine.

Fact 762: The African continent is the oldest populated area.

Fact 763: Dinosaurs lived on earth for 170 million years. In contrast, humans (Homo Sapiens) have only been around for 300,000 years.

Fact 764: The Marvel superhero Northstar, a French-Canadian mutant, was the first gay superhero in the world.

Fact 765: On average, a man ejaculates 7,200 times during his entire life.

Fact 766: Around the region of the Ecuadorian city of Quito, a large number of the inhabitants suffer from a special form of dwarfism. The genetic mutation which inhibits growth also protects those affected from all forms of cancer and diabetes.

Fact 767: At the age of five years and eleven months, Ayan Qureshi passed the "Microsoft Certified Professional Test", making him the youngest computer specialist in the world.

Fact 768: It takes the sun 226 million years to circumnavigate the Milky Way.

Fact 769: City birds are now integrating cigarette stubs into their nests as they have recognized that these are effective against insects.

Fact 770: The moonwalk was not actually invented by Michael Jackson. Cab Calloway included similar movements in his performances as early as 1932. At that time, however, people called it "The Buzz".

Fact 771: "Paruresis" is the fear that makes it impossible for people to urinate when other people are around.

Fact 772: On a flight from Amsterdam to Boston a woman from Uganda gave birth to a child. In the end, the baby was given Canadian citizenship as it was born in their airspace.

Fact 773: Babies are not able to taste salt until they are four months old.

Fact 774: During the Olympic Games in China, Usain Bolt ate only chicken nuggets, as it was the only meal he recognized from home. Ultimately, he won three gold medals with this diet.

Fact 775: Toilet paper was invented in China in the 13th century.

Fact 776: Karl Marx named all four of his daughters Jenny after his wife Jenny Marx.

Fact 777: Termites eat their food at double the speed when heavy metal is played.

Fact 778: There is a type of fungus that grows on ants and controls their behavior. The ant then has no control over its own body.

Fact 779: At Starbucks "laughing" is part of the job description.

Fact 780: The drug lord Pablo Escobar had so much cash in his home that rats ate about a billion dollars of his wealth per year.

Fact 781: Octopi have three hearts.

Fact 782: Because all passports in the UK are officially issued by the Queen, she does not own a passport. When travelling abroad she just has to state that she is the Queen.

Fact 783: While tomatoes are typically classified as vegetables, they actually belong to the fruit category.

Fact 784: The hair above a cat's eyes is called tactile hair.

Fact 785: The storming of the Bastille was mainly symbolic, at the time there were only nine prisoners who were subsequently freed.

Fact 786: The average age of soldiers fighting in Vietnam was 19. During World War II it was 26.

Fact 787: A bite of the Brazilian wandering spider can cause men an erection that lasts for hours.

Fact 788: In France, the national fencing federation recognized light saber fencing as an official competitive sport in 2019. Instead of saber, foil or sword, the fighters use replicas of light sabers from Star Wars. With this campaign, the association hopes to get more young people interested in fencing.

Fact 789: 450 men die of breast cancer in the U.S. each year.

Fact 790: The real name of the Michelin mascot is "Bibendum" or "Bib" for short.

Fact 791: Between 2009 and 2012, Alexander Bychkow killed and ate at least nine people. According to him, he did this to impress his ex-girlfriend, who had ended the relationship prior to the killings.

Fact 792: In the last 3,000 years, there were only 268 years in which no wars occurred.

Fact 793: A piece of biscuit that survived the sinking of the Titanic was auctioned for over 15,000 pounds. The biscuit was 103 years old at the time.

Fact 794: Robert Williams, a former Ford assembly line worker, was the first human to be killed by a robot. He was fatally hit in the head by a robot arm in 1979.

Fact 795: The first Google Doodle was the Google logo including a Burning Man stick figure and came out on the 30th of August 1998. The intention for it was to show everybody that both founders Page and Brin attended the festival.

Fact 796: So far, there have already been around 106 billion people in the world.

Fact 797: In the Middle Ages green was the colour of love.

Fact 798: The national animal of Scotland is a unicorn.

Fact 799: In 1993, Canadian lawyer Garry Hoy wanted to prove to a group of visitors that the glass in the Toronto Dominion Centre was unbreakable. To demonstrate this, he jumped against the glass - which thereupon broke out of its frame and plummeted downwards together with Garry Hoy. Hoy died, but the pane of glass remained intact, even after the fall.

Fact 800: Japanese people believe that black cats bring good luck.

Fact 801: The phenomenon of having to sneeze when suddenly exposed to bright light is called the photic sneeze reflex.

Fact 802: About 75 percent of all people are scared of speaking publically in front of people.

Fact 803: The first person to give weather phenomena human names was the American Clement Wragge. He decided to name hurricanes after politicians in order to allow witty allusions to their political activities. The system has remained in place to this day.

Fact 804: The average distance a man walks on foot during his life is four times around the world.

Fact 805: The Japanese company YKK is the largest manufacturer of zippers in the world. That is why the company logo "YKK" can be found on most zippers worldwide.

Fact 806: When the space probes Rosetta and Philae left the earth on March 2, 2004, there were no iPhones, Facebook existed for 27 days and nobody knew of Twitter.

Fact 807: The maximum speed of a T.Rex was slower than the average sprinting speed of a human.

Fact 808: In 1994 the iPad would have been the fastest computer on earth.

Fact 809: Angela Merkel's middle name is Dorothea.

Fact 810: The longest boxing match in the world took place on 6 April 1893 between Andy Bowen and Jack Burke. The fight went on for 110 rounds and lasted for more than seven hours. In the end, both fighters were too tired and exhausted to keep on fighting.

Fact 811: Sleep researchers have confirmed that women need more sleep than men and are more likely to suffer health damage if they do not get enough sleep.

Fact 812: Celery has "negative" calories - it costs more energy to digest it.

Fact 813: The Nobel Prizes were established by the Swedish inventor Alfred Nobel. He invented dynamite and went on to become very wealthy because of it. Before dying, he drew up a will stipulating that after his death the majority of his assets were to go to his foundation. The interest generated from these assets is used to award annual Nobel Prizes in physics, chemistry, medicine, literature and peace efforts. They were first awarded in 1901.

Fact 814: The blue whale is the loudest animal on earth. Its cries can be heard from a distance of 373 miles.

Fact 815: McDonald's sells 75 burgers per minute.

Fact 816: Astronauts in the ISS can witness 15 sunrises and 15 sunsets a day.

Fact 817: Fingernails grow approximately four times faster than toenails.

Fact 818: Ten percent of all car accidents are caused by being distracted, for example when writing an SMS.

Fact 819: Studies show that people who live by the sea have lower levels of stress than others. Scientists suspect that the color blue may have a strong influence on stress levels.

Fact 820: In Surabaya, Indonesia, residents can also use plastic waste to pay for their bus ticket. The objective of the campaign is to reduce plastic waste in the city and at the same time get more people interested in public transport.

Fact 821: A koala's fingerprint is so similar to that of a human being that there have been several cases in Australia with considerable confusion about the perpetrator at a crime scene.

Fact 822: When her ship capsized in 1880, the former queen of Thailand, Sunandha Kumariratana, drowned together with her daughter. Despite the presence of many courtiers, no one dared to save the queen, as just a few years earlier it had been punishable by death to touch a member of the royal family.

Fact 823: In 1938, Adolf Hitler was Time Magazine's "Person of the Year".

Fact 824: The human eye reacts so well to light that it could see the flame of a candle in absolute darkness from about 30 miles away.

Fact 825: The two most common reasons for a bad temper are hunger and insufficient sleep.

Fact 826: When Ed Headrick, the inventor of the Frisbee, died in 2002, his ashes were melted down into Frisbees and distributed to his family and closest friends.

Fact 827: Finland was the first country in the world to make broadband Internet access a legal right. If a house does not have a broadband connection, a Finish tenant can sue his or her landlord or the city.

Fact 828: The "hyoid bone", a small bone in the oral cavity under the tongue, is the only bone in the human body that is not connected to another bone.

Fact 829: The Counter Strike team "Silver Snipers" consists of five members who are between 62 and 81 years old.

Fact 830: The most common first name in Italy is Russo.

Fact 831: Marie Byrd Land in Antarctica and Bir Tawil, an area between Egypt and Sudan, are the only areas in the world that do not belong to a nation. These areas are therefore no man's land.

Fact 832: The longest mathematical proof is more than 15,000 pages long and was written by more than 100 mathematicians.

Fact 833: In remembrance of the deceased actor Paul Walker, Vin Diesel named his daughter "Pauline".

Fact 834: The Tetris effect, or Tetris syndrome, is the phenomenon that occurs when a person spends so much time on an activity that it affects all of their thinking, visual perception and even their dreams. So people who have played too much Tetris often dream of falling blocks or try to bring more order into all areas of their lives.

Fact 835: The medicine Imatinib is used to treat leukemia and costs 65,000 dollars for a year's supply. In India the same medicine is available for 2,500 dollars a year, because the pharma company could not patent it there.

Fact 836: After watching the series "Breaking Bad", Hannibal actor Anthony Hopkins wrote a letter to Bryan Cranston, the main character of the series, and told him: "Your performance as Walter White was the best acting I have seen - ever".

Fact 837: The word "mafia" refers to the criminal organization in Sicily. Comparable structures in other regions use their own names like "Camorra" or "Yakuza".

Fact 838: The Bonobo Kanzi monkey is able to make its own bonfire and cook its food in it.

Fact 839: In 1980 a hospital in Las Vegas had to dismiss several employees as they were betting on when patients would die.

Fact 840: The first seven seconds are the most important when making a first impression.

Fact 841: The most common languages in Africa are Arabic, English, Swahili, French, Berber, Hausa, Portuguese and Spanish.

Fact 842: In Alaska there is a sand desert with dunes up to 160 feet high.

Fact 843: For years, Liechtenstein and Haiti had the same flag, which was only noticed when the two nations met at the 1936 Olympic Games. A year later, the flag of Liechtenstein was therefore adorned with the symbol of a golden princely hat.

Fact 844: google.com is the only website that maintains that users should spend as little time on it as possible.

Fact 845: It takes over 15 million Lego bricks to re-create everything from "The Lego Movie".

Fact 846: When the USA bought Alaska from Russia in 1867, they switched from the Julian calendar previously used in Alaska to the Gregorian calendar used in the USA. The result was that the 8th to 17th of October 1867 never existed in Alaska.

Fact 847: Some roads in Australia are so long that the Australian state counteracts the risk of fatigue by playing little trivia games with the drivers along the side of the road.

Fact 848: The children of the nephews of Adolf Hitler had voluntarily sterilized themselves, in order for the Hitler bloodline to become extinct.

Fact 849: In 2017, Ed Sheeran paid more taxes in the UK than Amazon and Starbucks.

Fact 850: The world's first vibrator was patented in 1869 and was powered by a small steam engine.

Fact 851: One million seconds correspond to about twelve days, while one billion seconds correspond to 32 years.

Fact 852: In the Simpsons, God and Jesus are the only characters with five fingers.

Fact 853: In order to better investigate the effects of a black widow's poison, the scientist Allan Walker Blair voluntarily let the dangerous spider bite him.

Fact 854: Vin Diesel invested 3,000 dollars to produce the film "Multi Facial". The film was about his problems getting a real major role. Steven Spielberg watched the movie and cast Vin Diesel for his first major role in "The Soldier James Ryan". From then on his career began.

Fact 855: The younger you look for your age, the higher the likelihood to live for a long time.

Fact 856: There are currently more than 28 million miles of photographed roads in Google Street View available.

Fact 857: In China there is an app where you can order a "gangster", who can take care of your "enemies".

Fact 858: About 99,99999999999% of an atom is "nothing". If one would eliminate the empty space of all atoms from the entire human race, the remaining mass would fit in a coffee mug.

Fact 859: The boxing ring is called a "ring" because it used to be round. Instead of its present form, the spectators used to stand in a circle around the fighters when the sport first became popular.

Fact 860: Since Penélope Cruz was pregnant during the shooting of "Pirates of the Caribbean: On Stranger Tides", her sister Mónica Cruz, who is three years younger, stepped in as her body double.

Fact 861: The vertical groove that runs from the nose to the center of the upper lip is called "philtrum".

Fact 862: For his role as Iron Man, Robert Downey Jr. was paid 500,000 dollars in the first part. For the first Avengers film, however, his pay had already increased to 50 million dollars.

Fact 863: Male narwhals have an ivory horn with a length of up to ten feet on their head.

Fact 864: In 1923, a dead rider finished first in a horse race in New York. The rider suffered a heart attack during the race and the horse carried the dead body to the finishing line.

Fact 865: A study has shown that four percent of all people dream exclusively in black-and-white.

Fact 866: In Cambridge (Canada) you can pay your parking ticket by donating soft toys.

Fact 867: The smell of rain on dry earth is called "petrichor".

Fact 868: Venus rotates around its own axis at only four miles per hour. So you could walk around Venus faster than it can turn itself.

Fact 869: Sharks have been living on our planet for more than 420 million years. They existed before the dinosaurs.

Fact 870: The highest temperature ever measured in a human body was 115.7 degrees Fahrenheit.

Fact 871: The spider species "Caeristris darwini"spins the largest webs in the world. Their size can reach more than ten feet.

Fact 872: In Japan, a restaurant called "The Restaurant Of Order Mistakes" was opened. The restaurant's waiters all suffer from dementia, so visitors never know if they will really get what they ordered.

Fact 873: Scientists have succeeded in creating a genetic strain of manioc that contains more iron and zinc than conventional plants of this type. The crop is a widespread food source, particularly in Latin America, and with this special breeding it could reduce the problem of zinc and iron deficiency in children within the region.

Fact 874: A newborn has just 234 milliliters of blood in its body.

Fact 875: The parrot "Alex" remains the only animal to ever have asked a question. When he was shown a mirror, he asked, "What color?"

Fact 876: Shortly before his death, James Barrie, the creator of Peter Pan, transferred the rights to his book to the Great Ormond Street Hospital in London, which today is one of the leading children's hospitals in Britain. To this day, the royalty income from the book continues to support the hospital in treating a large number of children.

Fact 877: The Pomato is a hybrid between a tomato and a potato. The plant produces both tomatoes and potatoes.

Fact 878: The largest volcano in the world - the Tamu Massif in the Pacific - has an area roughly the size of Great Britain and Ireland combined.

Fact 879: The unit of one "meter" was first introduced during the French Revolution and was defined as one ten-millionth of the distance between the North Pole and the equator.

Fact 880: It has been known since 1971 that the Olympus Mons volcano on Mars is the largest known volcano in our solar system. By comparison, it was not until 2013 that the largest volcano on Earth was discovered: the Tamu Massif in the Pacific.

Fact 881: "K'o K'ou K'o Lê", the phonetically correct Chinese translation for Coca-Cola, literally means "A female horse fastened with wax".

Fact 882: Almost 90% of all cases or malaria worldwide occur in Africa.

Fact 883: You need at least 17 given numbers in a Sudoku to ensure there is a single, unambiguous solution.

Fact 884: When we talk to somebody we like, our voice changes.

Fact 885: Jim Cummings, the voice of Winnie Pooh in the U.S., regularly calls seriously ill children in hospitals and talks to them in his Winnie Pooh voice to delight them.

Fact 886: The fuel of a Nazi V2 rocket was produced from 33 tons of potatoes – so-called potato schnapps.

Fact 887: From a logical point of view, you can spend the rest of your life without taking even one more breath.

Fact 888: Twelve newborn babies are given to false parents every day.

Fact 889: If you cook a penguin egg, the egg white remains transparent after cooking.

Fact 890: In 2016, Pizza Hut delivered a pizza to the top of Kilimanjaro, setting the world record for the highest pizza delivery ever.

Fact 891: The human heart beats more than 100,000 times a day.

Fact 892: You can't commit suicide by holding your breath.

Fact 893: American Steven Pruitt has written over 30,000 articles on Wikipedia and improved over three million articles. This corresponds to about one third of all articles available on Wikipedia in English. In 2017, Time magazine therefore named him one of the 25 most influential people on the Internet, along with Donald Trump, J. K. Rowling and Kim Kardashian.

Fact 894: In addition to the known blood types of the AB0 system, there is a fourth, very rare variant. It is colloquially called the Bombay blood group, since only about 20,000 people worldwide have this blood group, almost all of whom come from India.

Fact 895: The fear of long words is called hippopotomonstrosesquipedaliophobia.

Fact 896: Bob Marley's wife Rita was shot in the head in an assassination attempt in 1976. Due to the thickness of her dreadlocks, however, she survived the incident.

Fact 897: In Texas, there is a city called Earth; it is the only place in the world named "Earth".

Fact 898: Scientists believe that it is possible to exterminate all mosquitoes, without impacting on our global ecosystem.

Fact 899: Based on an interview, Pope Francis watched television for the last time on the 15 July 1990.

Fact 900: The vagina has a self-cleaning mechanism.

Fact 901: Because Donald Duck doesn't wear pants, his comics were banned in Finland for a long time.

Fact 902: The often mentioned "Bro Code" and "Playbook" are real books, which can be bought.

Fact 903: Every year, humans kill up to 100 million sharks to get to their fins.

Fact 904: Santa Claus was not invented by Coca Cola.

Fact 905: Just like whales, elephants and hippos can communicate with their fellow creatures over long distances via infrasound.

Fact 906: The deepest species ever found is the devil worm (Halicephalobus mephisto). It was discovered in a cave in South Africa 2.2 miles underground.

Fact 907: The largest dog in the world is 43.7 inches tall.

Fact 908: Humans do not develop exclusively through the genetic mixture of mother and father. On average, every human is born with about 100 mutations.

Fact 909: Of the 195 countries in the world, there are only 22 countries that have never been attacked or occupied by Britain.

Fact 910: A fully-grown elephant can drink about 53 gallons of water within five minutes.

Fact 911: Rhnull (rhesus factor zero) is the rarest blood type in the world. So far, only 40 people worldwide are known to have this blood group.

Fact 912: The largest shark that ever lived was the Megalodon. It could grow to a length of up to 65 feet, almost three times the size of a white shark.

Fact 913: Popeye has four nephews named Pupeye, Pipeye, Peepeye and Poopeye.

Fact 914: All people begin their lives as females. The male Y chromosome becomes active just after the fifth week of gestation.

Fact 915: On 1 April 2017, Pornhub played a very special April fool's prank on its users. After they had clicked on a video, a picture with the message "Thanks for Sharing - Pornhub now has automatic video sharing to your social media accounts" was displayed.

Fact 916: Brooklyn "Brookie" Supreme is considered the largest horse to ever have existed. It was almost 6.6 feet tall and weighed over 1.5 tons.

Fact 917: When in England the packaging of the drug Tylenol was changed from a bottle to a blister pack, the suicide rate involving the drug decreased by more than 50 percent. Instead of taking several tablets out of the container at once, each tablet had to be squeezed out of the blister pack individually, giving people more time to reconsider their suicide attempt.

Fact 918: The name "Google" is derived from the word "googol" which denotes a one followed by one hundred zeros.

Fact 919: Frequent sex increases the growth of brain cells.

Fact 920: Originally, Grand Theft Auto was meant to be a racing game named "Race'n'Chase" but a glitch made police cars ram into the car of the player. This element was so popular with the game testers that a whole game was modelled on this principle and GTA was born.

Fact 921: A study conducted by Oxford University in 2009 showed that playing Tetris after a traumatic event can significantly improve trauma management.

Fact 922: The Titanic II is scheduled to put to sea in 2022, following the route of the original Titanic.

Fact 923: Pizza Hut was the first pizza service to deliver a pizza to the International Space Station. In 2001, the company paid one million dollars to the Russian Space Agency for this promotional campaign.

Fact 924: The "Book of Mormon", the religious foundation of the Mormon faith, which is close to Christianity, tells of a colonization of America in the time of Christ. The country is described as having always been rich in food and animals. Among other things, cattle, sheep, horses, pigs, goats, elephants, wheat and barley are mentioned. According to the latest scientific findings, however, these things only came to America with the colonization by Columbus.

Fact 925: Popcorn has been around since 3,600 BC.

Fact 926: The album "Hybrid Theory" by Linkin Park is the most sold debut album of the 21st century.

Fact 927: According to Bill Gates, just a small amount of poor countries will exist in 2035.

Fact 928: The reflex that we automatically lead a small wound to our mouth is an innate protective mechanism. The saliva in our mouth helps the blood to coagulate and kills bacteria.

Fact 929: Ice cream manufacturer Ben & Jerry's has a cemetery for discontinued ice cream varieties on its premises.

Fact 930: Cats cannot taste sugar.

Fact 931: The Jewish boxer Salamo Arouch was imprisoned in a concentration camp during World War II and was forced to fight against other inmates. The loser was shot or gassed.

Fact 932: Orthocarbonic acid is also known as "Hitler's Acid", as its graphic representation resembles a swastika.

Fact 933: A duel with three participants is called a truel.

Fact 934: In the past, the sickrooms of cancer patients were always round, as there was a superstition that cancer cells always gathered in the corners of rooms. To this day, you can still find many historic hospitals with round rooms.

Fact 935: Algeria is not just the largest country in Africa but also among the then largest countries in the world.

Fact 936: Since 1896, soccer fields in Germany have to be free of trees.

Fact 937: The longest street in the world connects Alaska with the south of Argentina. It has a length of approximately 18,641 miles and crosses 17 states, six time zones and four climate zones.

Fact 938: Dogs are red-green blind.

Fact 939: Most "Converse" sneakers have a small piece of felt on the sole, which usually comes off after wearing the shoe for the first time. The reason for this is that due to the piece of felt, the shoes are officially categorized as house shoes and therefore carry lower import duties.

Fact 940: The female form of the Indian-Hindu ruler's title "Maharajah" is "Maharani".

Fact 941: Henry Ford was the first tycoon to not let his employees work on Saturdays and Sundays, so that they could spend more time with their cars. Thus the weekend was born.

Fact 942: Dogs and humans are the only mammals with a prostate.

Fact 943: In the 1960s, the Barbie model "Slumber Party Barbie" was released, which gave children extra tips on how to lose weight. One of them was that you should not eat anything.

Fact 944: The word "Swagger" is a neologism and was created by William Shakespeare.

Fact 945: When you obtain a doctorate in Finland, you receive a hat and a sword from your university.

Fact 946: The Swedish word for stepmother is "Bonusmamma".

Fact 947: In 2010, General Electrics made profits of 14 billion dollars and paid not a penny in taxes.

Fact 948: It is assumed that the pizza Hawaii was invented in Canada.

Fact 949: In 1954 Bob Hawke, the future prime minister of Australia, set the world record by drinking 2.5 liters of beer in 11 seconds.

Fact 950: In Italy on New Year's Eve, traditionally one wears red underwear to have luck for the new year.

Fact 951: There is a Barbie doll which is modelled after Angela Merkel.

Fact 952: In the early 1980s, Pablo Escobar was responsible for 80 percent of the world's cocaine production.

Fact 953: To celebrate its 50th birthday, around 300,000 people crossed the Golden Gate Bridge simultaneously on 24 May 1987. This resulted in the bridge sinking by 3.2 feet.

Fact 954: Humans are the only species that cook their food.

Fact 955: The people who voiced Mickey Mouse and Minnie Mouse in the 1930s were married in real life.

Fact 956: In May 2015, 2.3 million Americans were still logging on to the Internet using a 56k modem and an old AOL access.

Fact 957: Current research assumes that Jesus was not born on 25 December, but rather in March. So instead of commemorating Jesus Christ at Christmas, we should instead honor Isaac Newton, who was verifiably born on 25 December.

Fact 958: The Sahara is not just the largest desert in the world but also bigger than mainland USA.

Fact 959: The first virtual reality cinema has already opened its doors in Amsterdam. Visitors can swivel their chairs to enjoy a 360-degree-view of the film.

Fact 960: With one "bite", blue whales consume up to 1,100 pounds of food or almost half a million calories. Opening the mouth and eating food alone can burn up to 2,000 calories.

Fact 961: The founders of Adidas and Puma were brothers.

Fact 962: The first ATMs required six digits as a PIN. However, after a large number of users could not remember six digits, the PIN was reduced to four digits.

Fact 963: The Bluetooth logo is composed of the old Nordic runes for H and B, which were the initials of Viking king Harald Bluetooth. He was known for his overwhelming communication skills.

Fact 964: Bruce Banner - the Hulk's alter ego - holds seven doctorates.

Fact 965: The saying "Happy wife, happy life" has been scientifically proven. Men whose wives are happy are also happier themselves.

Fact 966: If you had invested $100 in Bitcoin in 2010, you'd be worth more than $70 million now.

Fact 967: In 2007, Navy SEAL Mike Day was shot 27 times by four al-Qaeda leaders. He managed to kill the four leaders and get himself to safety. Today, he is in good health again and lives happily with his wife and daughter.

Fact 968: Papua New Guinea is the country with the greatest variety of languages spoken in a single country. Although the country has only about eight million inhabitants, more than 700 different languages are spoken.

Fact 969: Super Mario was originally a carpenter before he was portrayed as a plumber in later parts of the series.

Fact 970: After being hit by an avalanche, the arctic scientist Peter Freuchen freed himself by making a chisel from his frozen stool. After this, he amputated his frostbitten toes with a hammer.

Fact 971: In the British Army only soldiers ranked "Pioneer Sergeant" are allowed to have a beard.

Fact 972: The U.S. channel Fox has the rights on the Simpsons until 2082.

Fact 973: In 1983 Marvel released a comic series called "Spider-Pig". The main character was "Peter Porker".

Fact 974: September always begins on the same day of the week as December.

Fact 975: The Hungarian psychologist László Polgár put forward the theory that every human being can be educated to become a genius if only you start encouragement early enough. He convinced his wife of the idea and taught his three daughters chess at the age of four. All three daughters reached the rank of Grand Master. One of the daughters became the second-best female chess player in the world - behind her sister Judit Polgár, who even rose to become the world's best female chess player. Overall, she ranked eighth worldwide.

Fact 976: The first flags of pirates were red, not black.

Fact 977: The Cristo Redentor statue in Rio de Janeiro is not the largest Christ statue in the world. With a height of 108 feet, the Christ the King statue in Poland is ten feet higher.

Fact 978: Because intelligent people think faster, their handwriting is sloppier.

Fact 979: The "Antarctic Treaty" signed in 1961 stipulates that no country may exploit Antarctica economically or use it militarily. Instead, Antarctica is to be made available to all countries of the world for research purposes.

Fact 980: On Jupiter and Saturn it rains diamonds.

Fact 981: Female lions carry out 90 percent of the lion's hunting activities.

Fact 982: Only a few special types of piranhas eat meat. All others feed on plants.

Fact 983: Vladimir Putin once tried to exploit Angela Merkel's fear of dogs. The two heads of state met in Sochi in January 2007 to discuss important issues related to energy policy and cooperation between Russia and the EU. During the entire conversation, Putin let his Labrador "Koni" stay close to Merkel's legs.

Fact 984: As the earth rotates slower around the sun from year to year, 2016 was one second longer than 2015.

Fact 985: It was only in 1990 that the World Health Organization (WHO) officially ceased to regard homosexuality as a mental illness.

Fact 986: Ben Affleck was banned for life from playing at Hard Rock Casino in Las Vegas after security caught him counting cards while playing Blackjack.

Fact 987: During the Second World War, the city of Constance was largely spared from Allied bombing raids. Unlike other German cities, Constance did not cut off electricity at night. Allied pilots could therefore hardly distinguish the city from neighboring Switzerland, where the lights also remained on at night. In order to avoid mistakes, no bombs were dropped in the region.

Fact 988: The most popular quotes from Barney Stinson from "How I Met Your Mother" are "Have you met Ted?", "Wait for it", "What up" and "Suit up" and are already mentioned in the first episode of "How I Met Your Mother".

Fact 989: Chris Putnam is a developer at Facebook and has immortalized himself in social networks. If one writes :putnam: in a comment, one will see his face as a smiley.

Fact 990: In war times significantly more boys than girls are born. This is called the "Returning Soldier Syndrome".

Fact 991: In 1991 Dubai had only one skyscraper. Today, there are more than 400.

Fact 992: In 1967, Lawrence Roberts, one of the forefathers of the Internet, was still of the opinion that the exchange of messages among network participants was not an important motive for building a network of computers. Today, services such as WhatsApp, Telegram and e-mail have become an indispensable part of our everyday lives.

Fact 993: On average, people laugh ten times a day.

Fact 994: The term "Checkmate" comes from the Persian phrase "Shah Mat" which means "the king is dead"

Fact 995: Male clownfish become females when their partner dies.

Fact 996: There is a skeleton of a Tyrannosaurus Rex on the Google campus. It is supposed to remind employees not to let Google die out.

Fact 997: In 1957 a senior woman had to be brought out of a baseball stadium after being hit in her face by a baseball. When the paramedics were carrying her out, a second ball hit her.

Fact 998: Lake Karachay in Russia has been overrun with so much nuclear waste after World War II, that one hour of exposure is a lethal dose of radiation.

Fact 999: Babies are born with 300 bones. In adulthood this number decreases to 206.

Fact 1000: The capital of Kazakhstan is Astana. Which when translated means "capital".

www.ingramcontent.com/pod-product-compliance
Lightning Source LLC
Chambersburg PA
CBHW031250250726
48655CB00005B/2147